DREAM TO THE EXTREME

FAILURE IS NOT AN OPTION

D. GATHERIGHT

WESTBOW
PRESS®
A DIVISION OF THOMAS NELSON
& ZONDERVAN

WestBow Press books may be ordered through booksellers or by contacting:

WestBow Press
A Division of Thomas Nelson & Zondervan
1663 Liberty Drive
Bloomington, IN 47403
www.westbowpress.com
1 (866) 928-1240

ISBN: 978-1-5127-8480-0 (sc)
ISBN: 978-1-5127-8481-7 (e)

Library of Congress Control Number: 2017906233

Print information available on the last page.

WestBow Press rev. date: 05/12/2017

CONTENTS

Acknowledgements:

I would like to use these words to express how much I love and appreciate God for His wisdom in helping me to create this book. Therefore, all praise and honor goes to God the Creator for helping me pen these words. Gabrielle Gatheright my best friend, partner for life and awesome wife encouraged me to continue God's desire for this book to be completed. Yes, I thank God for my wife and her encouragement. My wife was and continues to be "my spark in the dark" especially when I doubted myself, and God's mission for the completion of this project. The smiles of victory from my bright flowers of sunshine Denisya, Dennis II, Gabriella, and Gabriel my wonderful children which all played a part and have a special place in my heart, and their memories I will forever cherish. My mom and dad who provided me with loving childhood memories that will never perish, because of the beat ups to success and how they did not tolerate any mess. To my brothers and sisters Joseph, Kenya, David, Terrance, Timothy, Latorris, LaMark, Judy, Alonzo, Kris, Katherine, Lisa, and Benny who believed and prayed for their brother. In loving memories of my deceased brothers Jimmy Jr, Alvin, Calvin, Anthony Gatheright and all the ancestors that have gone ahead of me. My Gratitude and appreciation goes to the Diocesan Bishop Jerry Jones, my pastor, who encouraged me to expand my vision. His wife, the assistant pastor, Ambassador, Evangelist first Lady Laverne Jones and the entire Apostolic Assembly family that supported and encouraged my spiritual growth.

To the late Bishop R. Price Jr founder of the Victory Orthodox Apostolic church in Chicago, and the current pastor Bishop Robert McKinstry. I am so grateful for the Illinois State Council and the Pentecostal Churches of the Apostolic Faith (PCAF) that inspired all of my writings in its own unique way. Special thanks go out to Ms. Lee Ann Thornton which deposited a seed into this project, also the Chicago Public Schools which has allowed me to work with some awesome children for the last fourteen years. Also my new family the Crete-Monee Educational center where I am currently employed. To Dr. Michael James, Norman Moore II, Austin Nelson, Mike & Vivian Whitted, Randy Saddler, Less Illedge, William Rogers, Greg Burton, William Burton, Johnny Townsel, Percy Jackson Sr, Steve Williams, Donald Cassell, Christopher Short, Willie Jones, Pastor David Settles (didn't forget you friend) All the Apostolic Assembly brotherhood and the Kings Men ministries, all these individuals encouraged me throughout this journey. I thank all my family, friends and loyal supporters that have helped me take my **Dream to the Extreme.**

INTRODUCTION (DREAMING)

Inside every one of us is a soul which is the Creator's creative expression that is stamped in us. This connects to the ambitious and motivated inspired side of us that when we want something bad enough we will stop at nothing to get it. How can we activate this side of us on an everyday basis? What can we do to take our dreams to the Extreme and not allow them to be like Langston Hughes calls a "dream deferred" that might "fester like a sore and then run"? Where do we start to become pushy with our ambitions and ruthless in a positive way, to do what we have to do to get the job done? Can this hunger that is bubbling inside of us never be quenched with a "no that is not for me" thought? When do we turn on this determined switch, and keep it on and never let it stop again? Is it possible to allow our dreams to be a reality or is the nightmare the actuality that becomes the truth daily in our lives? The million dollar question is, can our dreams become more than an idea in our brain?

As we explore this question in the pages of this book the reality is, that inside all of us there is an internal switch. This switch comes on when we desire or crave something and make up our minds that we have to have it, automatically what we say becomes a reality. Before we go on, let's think about our last conquest, maybe it was positive maybe it was negative. Let's take some time and jot down the steps that we took to grab it, seduce him or her, surrender to the pleasure, or just reach a goal or deadline.

The question we must ask ourselves is did we want to accomplish the goal and what did we do to make the dream become reality? If yes is the answer, which it is, let's start with the first process: desire. As we keep this desire in mind, please let "yes you can" be the focus as this book is read. With these goals and ambitions in mind our thinking just be abstract but focused on what we want to accomplish daily. Again let's think about our last successful endeavor, first we concentrated on what it took to own it. This desire led us to commit to certain practices. Once we commit to it we became consistent with achieving this desire. The desire might not have taken long to fulfill, based on our desperation to have our need met or greed fed. However, once we did what we wanted to do our desire developed into creative energy. This began a process that helped our desire to materialize as successful results.

Now if we think about something resulted in failure if this never develops into manifestation. It never developed because at some point we lost the desire. Distractions kept us from committing to a consistent effort, because our goal was abandoned for something else. Yet, there is a yearning in us all to never want to fail. This yearning calls for a continuance of achieving that which we see ourselves becoming. This creative energy stays within us until we die. Those that have ignored it walked a road in life that led to depression or a state of high anxiety. There is a successful principle related to everything. In this book we will explore the successful principle that comes with a peace that can only be found in the creative word of God.

This creative word must become activated in us. Jesus is an example of how the creative word can cause us to accomplish our goals. Jesus came to fulfill the law that guarantees we are no longer bound to defeat. This is a very easy statement to say but very difficult to portray because the flesh wars against the spirit and the spirit against the flesh. Once we are baptized in the water and the spirit our negative past behavior is finished. Jesus looked to the heavens on the cross at Cavalry and declared the end to the curse of man, which is death. However once a person is born of the water and spirit, he or she can live in the newness of life and have peace from the torment of everyday struggles. Money cannot buy happiness, and peace only comes from the creator of peace and not the author of lies.

There is a way that appears right to man but the end thereof is death.

Proverbs 14:12

Death leads to the termination of our existence with our life source forever if we don't make radical changes. We must make ourselves follow Christ's teachings and practices. The flesh never makes a transformation, but the spirit man reconnects with the true source that has the power to overcome the flesh. The true source is Jesus and He has all power in heaven and earth in his hands. No longer can the past defeat our ambitions and have us feeling condemned because now we have the ability to forget, reach and press out of any mess.

This book is designed to help us understand that once we are baptized by the water, and the spirit in the name that is given unto men we are empowered to **Dream to the Extreme**. This name frees us from the attitude of "I don't care" which leads to a nightmare. Eternal death is separation from the Creator, and brings pain that many of us try to relieve ourselves of as quickly as possible. This is not a book designed to argue about religious beliefs but to help release our dreams. To achieve this we must let this mind be in us which was also in Christ Jesus. He acted with a purpose and desire to express the creative energy that is fighting to get out of us. The cross stopped the continual process of defeat that led us to hell on Earth and eternity. Also, this book will help us understand why we are more than conquerors through him that loves us. By identifying the dream that lasts forever we can successfully fight against the fleshly desires that distract us from everlasting life.

Finally, as these pages are turned we hope that these principles that can help us reach our various goals, will be learned. Once we continue to accomplish our goals consistently, we will be placed in the category of taking our dreams to the extreme. Remember what we put in life is what we are going to get out of life. Extreme acts exceed expectations. If we allow our mind to respond to faith and not fear, then we are backing our dreams with faith. These dreams come from God the creator. The opposite of this mindset fears our dreams and possibilities. Decisions we chose to act or react turns our dreams into reality. Once we reach a goal than we use the same method to reach the next goal. This method of success becomes a faith process, which consists of concentrating on the dream. Then we commit and become consistent with transforming this procedure into actuality. Our dreams can be achieved based on how we believe. Daily events activate fear or faith and based on our choice we accomplish our dreams or experience a nightmare.

FAILURE IS OVER

Comfort, comfort my people, says your God. Speak tenderly to Jerusalem, and proclaim to her that her hard service has been completed, that her sin has been paid for, that she has received from the LORD's hand double for all her sins. A voice of one calling: "In the desert prepare the way for the LORD; make straight in the wilderness a highway for our God. Every valley shall be raised up, every mountain and hill made low; he rough ground shall become level, the rugged places a plain. And the glory of the LORD will be revealed and all mankind together will see it. For the mouth of the LORD has spoken.

Isaiah 40:1-5

We work hard to reach a goal. This goal is often expressed by a long or short term objective. When a goal is reached there may be celebrations that include shouts of joy. There may be other times when the goal is abandoned and dreams are forgotten. How do we reach back and get that lost desire and remember that forgotten passion that once set our heart on fire? A renewed mind produces a mentality spoken about in Isaiah 40 helps us begin the process of retrieving that forgotten dream from the shelf. We must listen to comforting words in the worst of times which creates hope. Hope helps us to realize that our failures can be turned into successes. The message in this scripture is that Christ will pardon us of our iniquity based on His victorious accomplishment of being the one to pay for our mistakes. The first step toward abandoning and defeat and embracing victory is to repent of our past mistakes.

How can we succeed when we have failed over and over again? Surrendering to the victory process will always get us out of the mess. Once we surrender to success through faith, the glory of the Lord will be revealed as our dreams become a reality.

Finished is when something is over and has ended. We must understand that the past did not last, it's finished. We must keep this principle in mind. Understand we can do all things through Christ which strengthens us. Of course this applies to the born again believer, but anyone can have the power to unleash the successful beast that's inside. We have to know this; do we use faith or fear? Faith to trust God or fear to rely on methods that we think will work or make decisions based on scare tactics.

If we want what we are striving for to be forever than we need to get with the creator that is forever. If not we will become successful with our determination but eventually land into frustration because everything has a season. God has a reason which is for His glory to be revealed in our accomplishments.

How badly do we want to succeed? Is it a dying need and how do we proceed? Inside of us all is the breath of God that develops the creative energy we all possess. Adam was born in paradise in the Bible, and now we are searching for paradise. The amazing connection here is that Adam's disobedience caused him to be evicted from paradise, and our disobedience to God blocks us from entering into paradise. What does this have to do with the dream God has given us? Many of us take the creative energy and use it for selfish purposes and yes accomplish what we dreamed, but the Bible states what does it profit a man to gain the whole world and lose his soul? (Matthew 16: 26) Therefore, the dream that is from God should go back to God. This results in a peace that cannot be purchased or obtained by the many messages that come from others that declare happiness with desires that are very selfish. These desires include only us instead of the creative energy that comes from God with a peace that is waiting to be released in troubled minds. Our troubled minds need comforting. Once hope is established our creative ability develops. But when we are faced with making a choice do we become afraid or exercise faith? Now is the time to replace our fear with faith.

The hope that establishes this peace can be understood when we realize that the creator wants to create a paradise in our minds. This "mind" paradise can release the vision that fuels the dream that allows God's glory to be revealed in us. Jesus' purpose was to help us understand that our dreams come from a heavenly kingdom mind set. These thoughts do not register with the poverty that comes from this world's system. Jesus' mind added to our lives and never subtracted anything from us except those things that cause friction between us and God. Once this friction stops being a restriction, we move into the redemption process where the Bible declares:

> *They that trust in their wealth, and boast themselves in the multitude of their riches; None of them can by any means redeem his brother, nor give to God a ransom for him.*

> Psalm 49: 6-7

Redemption is necessary to bring us back in the position we were in when God breathed into man and he became a living soul. Now the creative energy that flows through us once we have been redeemed can help us dream to the extreme. Extreme is a tremendous excessive desire that drives us to the point of manifestation and this is necessary to overcome fleshly desires. We war with fleshly desires that lead to death, and if we don't repent by allowing the Holy Spirit to lead and guide us into all truth we will never understand why the wages of sin is death.

Sin is self-indulgence into nothing. When we indulge in nothing our dreams become a nightmare. The nightmare develops based on false promises that come from what we thought was right but the end result was the death to the dream or ambition being forever. If the choice is made to chase a lie, then our flesh grabs the temporary not the eternal. The Creator's energy creates for eternity, not for short term or fleeting moments. We obtain our desired results when we say yes to the creator and surrender to His will for our lives. Our dreams and the peace with our visions can exist if our daily behavior resists the lies and temptations of fleshly desires.

Only Jesus Christ, who is the creative energy, can give us the antidote to cure our poisonous thinking that flows through our blood stream that we inherited from Adam. However, when we accept Christ and surrender to his instructions for our life, we are free to believe as the scriptures have said that "out of our belly will flow rivers of living water". This water will develop into a mighty unleashing river in our minds also which if the ideas are followed up on we will be able to make our dreams a continuous experience. Let it be known that this river produces the joy that's necessary to follow the scriptures that open doors locked by man. Once the doors are open we can allow Jesus words, "be it unto us according to our faith" to become a reality in our lives.

We must understand that there are two type of desires; flesh and spirit. They both get results. The daily choices we make have the power to activate faith or fear. The frustration and temptation to walk away from spiritual goals develops when we accept the lies that cause us to obtain what we see based on fleshly desires. Fleshly desires deal with carnal and temporal experiences that develop into an addiction. Fear develops into a comfort zone that hinders progress. This fear challenges our faith and can be defined as a negative restriction that causes the dream to become a nightmare. It's very confusing because if we operate from desires that are dictated by our senses this can lead to frustration. However, if the spirit of God is leading and guiding us into all truth, we won't focus on desires that depress us because we are walking by faith. Walking by faith keeps as from responding to the fear generated by our senses.

The Bible declares:

> *For I know in me (that is, in my flesh,) dwelleth no good thing: for to will is to present with me; how to perform that which is good I find not. For the good that I would I do not: but the evil which I would not that I do.*

Romans 7:18-19

How badly do we want to perform the good in us? The answer is we want the results but do not want to put forth the effort because of the fear of leaving our comfort zone that comes from the desire within. Therefore it's necessary to take the dream to the extreme, so we can do the good that we really want to do and fight the evil that is present. We have a dream and it should not go to the grave with our physical body. We must have the faith to walk away from our comfort zone. This will allow our dream to be left as a legacy of our endeavors to allow good to overcome the evil in this world. We must fight this negative desire from within through faith in the creative word and not fear of it. The creative word will help us understand that although we may have failed in the past, but as we look to Jesus, the creative word of God it can lift us above the past defeat. This past defeat came from the fear from what has dwelled in us, but now we trust the creative word to redirect us to our dreams. The creative word declares that we are more than conquerors. This is the mentality we must have as we strive to make our spiritual dreams a reality.

Spiritual dreams must come with a spiritual desire and this yearning cannot be based on our five senses. What is the difference from a spiritual dream and a fleshly dream? In Isaiah 40:1, we see a prophet's vision whose dream was for his people (Israel) to be free of bondage. Out of his vision he speaks of a Messiah that will come to release his people from the heavy burden that is placed upon them by their task masters. The fear from what dwells inside of us that developed a comfort zone can be symbolized as our heavy task masters today.

> *Comfort ye, comfort ye my people saith your God, Speak ye comfortably to Jerusalem, and cry unto her, that her warfare is accomplished, that her iniquity is pardoned: for she hath received of the Lord's hand double for all her sins.*

Isaiah 40:1-2

Basically, it's finished which is the war in the mind to let go of our confidence we have placed in our comfort zone. The word of fear that triggers our senses that develops into negative behavior is over. Why is it over? The principle of replacing fear with faith is what we will use to take our dreams to the extreme. Our faith in the creative word will help us to stop listening to poisonous words that come to sabotage our success.

Isaiah mastered this principle by not relying on the comforting words of the flesh but the comforting words that came from the creator. Isaiah 40: 4-5 tells us about the Lord's coming and the fact that he would exalt every valley. He would bring down every mountain and hill; also make the crooked straight and the rough places plain. This creation is a source from the Creator and should cause us to have hope in dreams that have been abandoned and aspirations that have been forsaken. Through Jesus' acts and commitment to fulfill the will of the father, the glory of the Lord will be revealed. It takes a surrendered mindset with faith in the fact that when Jesus died on the cross for our sins, death and failure were finished. It's not by our works but our faith in the one that Isaiah had envisioned would come. John confirmed this in the New Testament when he declared: *"Behold the lamb of God which taketh away the sins of the world."* (John1:40)

Again sin is self-indulgence into nothing. All the wasted efforts and tireless moments of getting nowhere by our own strength ends when we surrender to the Creator. He is the one that can forever reestablish us to the internal desire that allows our dreams to become a positive reality. Not only do our dreams become a reality but we know how to use our dreams to bring stability to an unstable world. The spirit of God will lead us and guide us into all truth.

A DESIRE AND OPPORTUNITY

Let no man say when he is tempted, I am tempted of God: for God cannot be tempted with evil, neither tempteth he any man; But every man is tempted, when he is drawn away of his own lust, and enticed. Then when lust hath conceived, it bringeth forth sin; and sin, when it is finished, bringeth forth death.

James 1:13-15

Every behavior starts and ends with a desire. The Bible describes this as lust and enticement. However if the desire is for fleshly things, the end result is death. As we fulfill the desire for fleshly things a decaying usually takes place which results in death. This mindset should give us a mind to look at temptation or distraction as an opportunity. How can we look at temptation or distraction as an opportunity? We must desire to please God and not the flesh. The opportunity is dangling before us. We must not use it to think wrong, do wrong or just plain sin to sidetrack or block the revelation of God's glory. If we are to take our dreams to the extreme we must look to the author and finisher of our faith and not be drawn away by our carnal nature. Therefore, it takes the place as a distraction to the negative attraction which is the temptation that draws us away from God.

A desire combined with an opportunity either allows the flesh to be satisfied or God's glory to be revealed. Are we going to make life altering decisions based on faith in the creative word or fear generated by our natural senses? If flesh is satisfied then it won't be long before our dreams are put to death. We must understand that there are basic needs that trigger desires. Negative noise from a negative environment has us often thinking that our desires to meet these needs are essential to our growth. This can be the truth but we must remember every action is followed by a consequence.

If we intend to meet our needs and become satisfied, then we must trust the Comforter and not the deceiver. The Comforter is the Holy Spirit which leads and guides us into all truth. We must not be afraid to let the Comforter lead us into what may be new territory.

What is truth? The word of the Lord is truth. We must remember that the word of the Lord is the creative energy that guides us to the positive desire that adds, not subtracts from our dreams. The deceiver comes to make us think we have something when we really have nothing. If we are chasing what we see and connecting this to our aspirations in life these aspirations are like a hot air balloon that will burst. Our dreams must be birthed from the breath that was breathed into our nostrils that made us a living soul.

The tugging we feel from within is the dream that wants to manifest itself and the instructions for true manifestation comes from the creator of the soul. We must be careful to use faith to respond to this tugging and not fear. Our desire, when connected with what we see, leads us into the position where we are drawn away from the creator. This will connect with our lust that leads us to death instead of life. The world is confusing, and makes us think that dreams center around cars, women, money and houses. Nevertheless, the Bible declares, "what would it profit us to gain all this and lose our soul?" Our soul was birthed with the possibility of victory and not defeat. However, we must have a mindset that desires more of Christ. This mindset directs us down the path where we are used for the glory of the Lord. This mindset develops out of faith in God and fights the fear that comes from hearing and believing the world's definition of success and seeing the prosperity of the world.

> *That they all may be one; as thou, father, art in me, and I in thee, that they also may be one in us; that the world may believe that thou has sent me. And the glory which thou gavest me, I have given them, that they may be one even as we are one.*

> John 17:21-22

Jesus prayed this prayer that his disciples and those that came after his disciples might be one with him and the father. This reconnection takes place when we accept and act on his words. This allows us the opportunity to lay aside every weight that side-track us to rekindling fearful memories of our old desires. As we our challenged to fight the desire we must not be afraid to use faith to dream to the extreme.

Once we allow faith to control our behavior then the creator will allow the spirit of truth to lead us to our destiny. This process causes us to think higher than the world system that would subtract from the kingdom. Our negative desires lead us into bondage where it's all about us and our addictions. This restricts us from understanding that the creator has some glory that he wants to reveal. This glory will bring down the mountains that have developed from fear. This fear has developed into false appearances that seem impossible to climb. The crooked thinking is what the creator wants to straighten out and the rough places he will make plain. When this miracle takes place we have the knowledge that we can do all things through Christ which strengthens us. The world system is designed to reward a lucky few, but the creator's heavenly kingdom is designed to help everyone dream to the extreme. The creator wants us to use faith to replace the fears that have caused illusions to develop into rough places. The creative energy used to produce faith makes us one with the creative word. The benefits of being one with the word is our rough places become plain.

God's glory is the extreme that will lift us higher than the nightmare of past thoughts that punish and restrict us from the beauty that the creator wants us to enjoy on this earth. If we are choked with the negative poison of this world we will never have a feeling of autonomy and be free to pursue the goals we choose. Spiritual competence will be dwarfed and we will never meet the creators' standards that allow his glory to be revealed through us. The feeling of relatedness and connection with others will be caught up with a selfish "me, myself and I attitude." Jesus came to break that cycle and comfort us. His Holy Spirit helps us separate ourselves from a system that makes us dependent on it to identify our dreams.

Psychological freedom comes when we accept what Jesus said on the cross "It is finished". What's finished? Our mental mindset that says "no" wars against our inner motivation that says "Yes I can". The response of "no" has caused many of us to become stagnated and depressed. The creative energy does not accept "no" as a solution.

If we act without any fear of our past, which did not last, then our creative energy will find a way to go around the answer "no". We will be free to allow our dreams to manifest into action and become consistent with not settling for no. This causes our creative juices to flow.

I can do all things through Christ that strengthens me.

Philippians 4:13

No more; defeat, bad habits, wishful thinking, negative behavior, trusting a lie, crying over past mistakes, stagnation and procrastination, because we must get busy with the mindset to continue the work which leads us to our dream.

Father the hour is come; glorify thy son that thy son, also may glorify thee: As thou hast given him power over all flesh that he should give eternal life to as many as thou hast given him. And this is life eternal, that they might know thee the only true God, and Jesus Christ whom thou hast sent. I have glorified thee on the earth: I have finished the work which thou gavest me to do.

John 17:1-4

Now that Jesus has gone back to the Father and has accomplished what the word set forth to do, we have a guarantee that our dreams can become a reality. The word was sent on a mission and that mission was to speak life to the death. Now that the word has been spoken in our lives we have the power to say "no more." We must make up in our minds that once we quit, that's it, and know that Christ have given us power over our flesh. The flesh can no longer dictate what we will do because now we have life eternal through Jesus Christ. This life grants us the power and longevity to enjoy our dreams forever. This happens with a mind to glorify the Father by finishing the work he has given us to do. The key to what he has given us lies in our dreams. However; what will we trust; faith or fear to become a success? Do we have a mind stuck on something that is feared or will we allow the Lord to lead and guide us to all truth?

Jesus, the creative word of God, came on a mission similar to a heroic journey. His quest was to free man from the fear that came from being dominated by the flesh. Jesus was the word of God clothed in flesh. He was challenged by that flesh, but was not afraid to follow his Father instructions. He was challenged but he relied heavily on his mentor, which was his father. To conquer the challenge he would frequently visit heavenly realms through prayer and meditation. By praying and meditating he was successful in his mission to redeem man back to God. He returned home with all power in heaven and earth in his hand. What's the point?

> *Stand fast therefore in the liberty wherewith Christ hath made us free, and be not entangled again with the yoke of bondage.*

Galatians 5:1

> *Know ye not, that to whom ye yield yourselves servants to obey, his servants ye are to whom ye obey; whether of sin unto death, or obedience unto righteousness?*

Romans 6:16

He has empowered us to stand in the freedom that he accomplished through his mission on planet earth. We must realize now that our choice allows us to experience freedom or bondage. Freedom from the desire that hinders us from our dream or bondage that holds us hostage and dictates what we will do. Christ has freed us from ourselves and with this freedom we can be free from the hurt and pain.

DREAM KILLER

The realization is we can succeed yet there is a dream killer that is designed to kill dreams. The dream killer is fear which tries to make us believe that we can't succeed. This fear creates cognitive distortions. Cognitive distortions are defined as ways that our mind convinces us that something is true that really isn't.

The great deceiver uses our senses as weapons to attack the mind. Do we activate fear or faith when it comes to making decisions related to our dreams becoming a reality? Using our senses to guide us towards our destiny causes us to fall into the trap of self-indulgence into nothing.

This is the spirit's interpretation of nothing but the flesh believes it has something. The reality becomes evident with the length of time needed to achieve the desired goal. Self-Indulgence into nothing distorts our focus on how we set up goals for our life. How satisfying we were when we accomplished these goals? How long did that thrill and accomplishment last? Did it give us a desired result? What type of peace came from this accomplishment? Did accomplishing this goal give us some type of entitlement that developed into pride? How much did we lose to reach the goal?

This is where our mind convinces us of something that just isn't true. Our truth is based on our senses if we use fear, but our reality can be replaced by faith if we trust in the creative word of God. An example of this is in the Bible with the decision that was made in Genesis 3. God made everything and declared it was good. He then gave Adam and Eve instructions on how to enjoy paradise. God's instructions challenged Adam and Eve senses, which led to the fall of man.

> *When the woman saw that the fruit of the tree was good for food and pleasing to the eye, and also desirable for gaining wisdom, she took some and ate it. She also gave some to her husband, who was with her, and he ate it.*

Genesis 3:6

For all that is in the world, the lust of the flesh, and the lust of the eyes; and the pride of life, is not of the Father but is of the world.

I John 2:16

Studying these scriptures reveals that lust activates wrong behavior within us. Lust leads to death but if we are going to dream to the extreme we must crave for satisfaction that cannot die. We were designed to live forever and not die in our lust. Therefore, it's imperative that we trust that which is good and not fall for the lie. The lie is fed through a sense of fear.

Again our dream develops from what we do not see and if we focus on this Earth, we are into the lust of the flesh, the lust of the eyes and the pride of life. These are the weapons that are used to destroy our dreams. They are everyday distractions that many of us have been addicted to in one form or another. Do we focus on the dream daily or are we distracted by what we see, hear, touch, taste and smell? If yes, is the answer to our destiny then it's time to reevaluate what's more important the dream or the lust of the eyes or the pride of life. We automatically behave like Adam and Eve daily with thoughts that are spontaneous and develop from fear or faith. The fleshly thoughts appear valid but are associated with problematic behavior. The thoughts of faith appear unrealistic but according to the word of God are good thoughts, which come with peaceful results.

Therefore our goals should center on being mentally fit as we strive to be the best we can spiritually. Negative thinking subtracts from our dreams and positive thinking adds to our destiny. We may wonder how we can think positive thoughts when negative stimuli are all around us? Negativity creates thoughts that lead to feelings of depression or anxiety.

Let this mind be in you, which was also in Christ Jesus; Who, being in the form of God, thought it not robbery to be equal with God: but made himself of no reputation, and took upon him the form of a servant, and was made in the likeness of men: And being found in fashion as a man, he humbled himself, and became obedient unto death, even the death of the cross.

Philippians 2:7-8

He humbled himself. This attribute speaks volumes regarding the characteristics that will help us be disciplined enough to reach our destiny. Humility is being meek and not weak. According to Matthew 5:5 "the meek shall inherit the earth". Yes this can be interpreted many ways. By having a mind like Christ we should understand that Christ received all power in heaven and earth. This was the ultimate reward for his thinking. The point is, humbling ourselves yields positive results. Humility will allow us to stay focused on our dreams in faith and not through fear tactics from the flesh. The dream killers' goal is to fix our mind constantly on the distractions of the lust of the flesh, pride of life and the lust of the eyes. Do we act on fear of the flesh or faith in God? Being obedient unto death means being focused on our objectives to the point that we let nothing separate us from the Love of Christ. Christ's method of success was "I must do the will of him that sent me," Our motto should be "I must do the will of him that loved me." The Bible declares that there is no greater love than a man would lay down his life for his friends (John 15:15). It also mentions that we are his friends if we do what he says, and as we think today it often centers around what is in it for me mentality. The answer is an experience of joy, peace and happiness as we continue to put our trust in the master.

Therefore, by being obedient, we become purpose driven and understand responsibility comes with our decisions. The death on the cross for those that are aligning themselves with their dreams requires taking a mindset to die out to negativity. Negative thinking subtracts from our life and positive thinking adds to our life. The death on the cross is everything that will distract us from our responsibility to achieve what we believe. The Bible says *be it unto us according to our faith."* (Matthew 9:29)

In order to make our dreams a reality we must understand the principle of creation; that we create by thinking and following up on our thoughts with actions. Therefore, our thoughts must be positive or the dream killer will use negative thinking to subtract from our destiny.

> *Finally, brethren, whatsoever things are pure, whatsoever things are lovely, whatsoever things are of good report: if there be any virtue, and if there be any praise, think on these things.*

> Philippians 4:8

Value is defined as measured in usefulness and importance. This is how we view the ideas that the creator has engrained in our minds. Do we chase after these ideas every day? Can we say like Solomon, *"I found him whom my soul loves? "*(Song of Solomon 3: 4) How passionate are we towards not allowing anything to separate us from the Love of Christ? This love of Christ must be unstoppable and consistent with God's plan for our life. This will allow us the opportunity to be the necessary ingredient needed to guarantee our success. However, how much do we envision ourselves accomplishing small goals in order to reach the general objective? The point is many of us have so many questions that it keeps us from activating the courage required to act and come up with answers for ourselves.

> *By night on my bed I sought him whom my soul loveth: I sought him but I found him not. I will rise now, and go about the city in the streets, and in the broad ways I will seek him whom my soul loveth: I sought*

him, but I found him not. The watchmen that go about the city found
me: to whom I said, Saw ye him whom my soul loveth? It was but a
little that I passed from them, but I found him whom my soul loveth:
I held him and would not let him go, until I had brought him into my
mother's house, and into the chamber of her that conceived me.

Song of Solomon 3:1-4

Treating these scriptures as an action plan will stop the dream killer from stealing what we were created for. First, we must seek after that which our soul loves which is the idea implanted in our DNA. We must fight the fears that distract us from reaching our daily objectives. Diligently, we must seek after our dreams and do it daily because the lust of the flesh, pride of life and lust of the eyes can side track us from the road that leads to our destiny. In this passage of scripture, the narrator asks for answers to questions demonstrating someone that is actively going forth with a plan. We must ask ourselves, are we actively chasing after the things the creator has designed to be the components that will eventually cause us to say we found whom our soul loves?

The other category that we often find ourselves in is actively chasing something and once we obtain it we are not satisfied. This narrator was so excited about finding that which satisfied the soul that he held his love tight and was determined to not let it go. This is a secret that the dream killer does not want us to know; that when we connect with the giver of the dream our soul will be satisfied. Then we will hold on to it and not let go of our dream.

So I was great, and increased more than all that were before me in
Jerusalem: also my wisdom remained with me. And whatsoever mine
eyes desired I kept not from them, I withheld not my heart from any
joy; for my heart rejoiced in all my labor: and this was my portion of
all my labor. I looked on all the works that my hands had wrought, and
on the labor that I had labored to do: and, behold, all was vanity and
vexation of spirit, and there was no profit under the sun.

Ecclesiastes 2: 9-11

The key to keep in mind is that there is no profit, which is nothing of lasting value, under the sun. To take it a little farther, all that is in the world is the lust of the eyes, pride of life and the lust of the flesh. Again, this leads to vanity and vexation of the spirit. If lust becomes our trust, we will be driven to a point of despair which develops through disappointment that will cause us to doubt the creative energy that motivates us daily. The writer has concluded satisfaction is not to be found in natural things of this world.

Unfortunately, we live in a world that teaches just the opposite. This world is full of distractions that cause us to mentally kill out the creative side that wants to present us with joy everlasting. This cannot be attained through labor, but through trusting the creator to lead and guide us into all truth. Then we can be effective as we labor. Once this trust develops we hope with a feeling that something we desire is possible. The writer mentions how nothing was withheld from him, but as he envisioned his dreams it was manifested through his actions.

Therefore, the dream killer comes to steal, kill and destroy our hope. The Christian's hope knows that all things are possible to them that believe. The question that might arise is what should a Christian hope in? A Christian should hope in the manifested creative result that comes from the creator. Many successful people believe in their ideas despite what the negative forecast is predicting and overcome all odds to reach their goals. This is raw creative energy that is put into action through active participation in an idea that becomes a reality.

This same principle is true for the born-again believer, because they have been pushed into a state of desperation. When we become desperate we do desperate things. This is why the dream killer fights us so hard. The enemy to the dream wants us to lose hope in the promises of the creator. Our enemy knows that incoming information is channeled through automatic thoughts, and this is where the challenge takes place in the mind. Are these incoming thoughts channeled by fear or faith? Our mind is the seat of our emotions and we need to speak to those thoughts and *be not conformed to this world but be transformed by the renewing of our minds.* (Romans 12:1) Why must our minds be renewed? Solomon answers this in Ecclesiastes 2:11 where he comes to understand that all labor done under the sun is vanity and results in vexation of the spirit. This is based on the incoming thoughts that are channeled through automatic thinking, if it's not from the creator. Instead it's designed to destroy the creation. We must remember when God finished creating the world, he stated that it was good.

In the garden, Adam and Eve were tempted. Due to their curiosity and disobedience we have been taken captive by our desires. In psychological terminology, this is defined as an addiction. The addiction is replaced when we exercise our faith by surrendering our will to God's will. Once this transformation takes place we can dream to the extreme which is limitless with possibility. This produces peace that cannot come from world achievements.

Also, God's grace frees us from negative thinking that comes from the world. This type of thinking leads to depression and negative regression. His grace, which is sufficient, provides us with deliverance, so not only are our dreams achievable, but now miracles can be experienced daily.

A miracle is a phenomenal event that only comes from God, the creator. Upon exercising our faith we can create this mindset, so that we won't be vexed by efforts that the world promises with the fabrication of peace.

This faith develops when we replace our fears with faith in the miraculous power of God the creator. His favor is not fair. It sustains us when we make decision that challenges our hope. The creator is the one that establishes calm endurance under pressure which is patience.

> *Knowing this, that the trying of your faith worketh patience. But let patience have her perfect work that ye may be perfect and entire, wanting nothing.*

James 1: 3-4

We must be patient with our hope. Once this takes place we will be satisfied with the peace that comes from relaxing in the creator words. Again, as this world produces stimuli that trigger our thinking we must be patient with the word of the creator. Now we can fight to manifest the creative energy that wants to be released in our actions. The action of connecting to our purpose in life helps us arrive at the stage where we are not lacking but are connected with our life source. Once we make this connection, again all things are possible to him that believe. This will establish hope that what we desire is possible. The word of God states *"Which hope we have as an anchor,"* (Hebrews 6:19). This is what the dream killer is trying to remove, our stabilization in the creative energy that can manifest itself in our daily lives.

SELF-INDULGENCE INTO NOTHING

If we are fooled into believing that we can get something from nothing we will wind up with a void in our lives. Here a void is defined as an empty space which develops as a longing in all of us. Many mask this longing with self-indulgence into nothing. We spend a lot of time going after what we think can fill this empty space and neglect the dream that has been given to us by the creator. Fear stops us from using faith as a logical approach to reach our destiny and ultimately everlasting satisfaction. The Bible declares that *there is a way that seems right unto a man but the end therefore is death.* (Proverbs 16:25)

In order for us to act correctly, we must think about the actions and then behave accordingly. This is why it is so important for us to be led by a spirit of truth. Trusting what is within us is dangerous because it's understood and stated in the Bible that, *"And I know that nothing good lives in me, that is, in my sinful nature. I want to do what is right, but I can't."* (Romans 7:18, paraphrased)

If this spirit of truth is not leading us regardless of what we think, we are living a lie. Consequently, our dreams will become extinct and will never fulfill their purpose. When the desire is from the flesh, satisfying the flesh will lead to death. Death is the consequence for disobeying God.

Math teaches us that zero plus zero equals zero. Insanity can be defined repeatedly doing the same thing the same way and expecting a different outcome. This is the typical lifestyle of many going and going but having no care about the end result. This is a procedure that leads to a consequence that many have not carefully thought out. Self-preservation can be considered the first rule of survival for many, but a visionary sees more than self in their visions and seeks to be holistic in the process of obtaining the dream.

> *For God so loved the world that he gave his only begotten son, that whomsoever believeth in him should not perish, but have everlasting life.*
>
> John 3:16

The creator did not have selfish actions; therefore a message was sent to reconnect us to the creator. It was His Word which became flesh and dwelt among humanity.

16

So shall my word be that goeth forth out of my mouth: it shall not return unto me void but it shall accomplish that which I please and, and it shall prosper in the thing whereunto I sent it.

Isaiah 55:11

The results of an action cannot be argued against because this is what we experience. Reality living is facing facts which are generated from outcomes, and outcomes have to had been thought up first. Does what we think determine what we experience? Yes, the word of God is argued in many circles and fights have broken out concerning what this scripture says and what the other intend to express. For the sake of argument, we all have opinions but we cannot argue against the experiences and consequences that come with our choices. What does this have to do with the Lord's word leaving his mouth and not returning unto him void? Well this is how we achieve our dreams or self-indulge into nothing. Self-indulgence is a very addictive distraction. Remember many do it out of being afraid to disobey the desires of the flesh and leaving their comfort zone. Faith walkers disobey the flesh, obey God and live miraculous lives.

First, we must remain focused regardless of what we see, hear, smell, touch or taste because our dreams must be that important. If we are created by this awesome God then we should be able to get the same creative responses if we act based on faith in his word. Isaiah 55: 7-8 gives a format for how we can dream again and know that what we hope for is possible. If we forsake our indulgence into nothing and return to the creator He will abundantly pardon our sins. After this is done we are free of the entanglement in a lifestyle that produced tears, fears and less cheers. We must recognize that the creator's thoughts are higher than ours because of his love for humanity.

We must love humanity to the point that we love ourselves and not get tricked by human folly, because this can cause us to indulge into nothing. Once our thoughts become like the creator then all things are possible to us.

Since we live in a day where everything is complicated with data and research it might become hard to understand a solid definition of "nothing". Although the definition of nothing is nonexistence, this can become hard to wrap our minds around. Nothing defined as nonexistence is the promise that we receive from the liars of this world. This can only be determined by an experience and not a power point slide presentation from the latest self-help meeting.

A house can look gorgeous and full on the outside but on the inside it might be empty of all the necessities that are needed for it to be considered a home. Many live giving the outward appearance of happiness, prosperity and health, but inside of them are all of the characteristics and traits of a "happy life" are nonexistent. Only we know if we appear to have a life that is full but is really void on the inside. We know if what we have been chasing is like what Solomon describes in the Bible as vanity and vexation of the spirit through an experience. Is what we experience daily decided by faith or fear?

However, there is a dream that can fill that void, return us to our connection and help us to know all things are possible. We need this assurance when the storms of life come to challenge us to the point where we feel like screaming instead of dreaming. It's the vision that will keep us from perishing into a nonexistent category.

We must not be so ready to trust what we see, touch, taste, smell or hear because these are gateways to indulge into nothing. The creator declares that his word will lead and guide us into all truth. The truth is the word that will not return void because it's on a mission and does not have the time for distractions. The question we must ask ourselves is will we allow this spirit to lead and guide us to our destiny?

Our destiny is the experience that the dream killer wants to steal, kill and destroy. Reality living is to understand that every action has a consequence. What are we thinking when we have to make a choice? Is the choice based on fear or faith? Remember, in order to act we must put a thought into the behavior. If we want our actions to cause change we must first change our thoughts. We must have the mind of Christ if we intend to be exalted above the negativity in this world.

> *The word of God is quick, and powerful, and sharper than any two edged sword, piercing even to the dividing asunder of soul and spirit, and of the joints and marrow, and is a discerner of the thoughts and intents of the heart.*

> Hebrews 4:6

We must be careful not to act on every thought that crosses our mind. Prayer and meditation is important when it comes to making decisions, because there is a way that seems right but the end of that way is death.

SPIRITUAL IDENTITY THEFT

Now the works of the flesh are manifest, which are these: Adultery, fornication, uncleanness, lasciviousness, Idolatry, witchcraft, hatred, variance, emulations, wrath, strife, seditions, heresies, envyings, murders, drunkenness, reveling and such like: of the which I tell you before, as I have also told in time past, that they which do such things shall not inherit the kingdom of God.

Galatians 5:19-20

Identity is defined as to the condition or character as to who a person or what a thing is; this includes the qualities, beliefs and practices of identifying the person or thing. God created man in his image but because of the lustful desires of Adam and Eve, man decided to be like God and this lustful thinking was more promising than the image of God their creator. This fleshly image now redefines man in a false image that lives after the flesh. This is called spiritual identity theft, because we spend our waking moments chasing a fantasy and never accepting reality. Instead of being identified in the spiritual realm as empowered dreamers, we become recognized as habitual pleasers and flesh seekers that have neglected our destiny for temporal pleasures.

How does the process work? First, we must understand that this is a process that requires mental work. If we want the dream to be achieved, we must fight the fear that affects our thinking which comes to steal our creative identity and leave us to chase fantasies that come with empty promises. A schema provides the basis by which we relate to the events we experience. We identify with success and failure based on this thinking in our mind that's an underlying organizational pattern or structure; that is based on fear or faith. Fear suspends our destiny and faith releases our potential to fulfill our destiny. What does this have to do with spiritual identity theft? A famous quote sums up why we are living with a mistaken identity. "We are not human beings having a spiritual experience. We are spiritual beings having a human experience." (Pierre Teilhard de Chardin)

Unfortunately, the fear of not wanting to go against world views and popular opinion hinders us from bringing our spirituality into this human experience.

Spiritual identity theft comes through submitting to automatic thoughts that have produced experiences that come through allowing the flesh to work and not the spirit. If this continues we are putting ourselves at risk to be emotionally vulnerable to various emotions that come with an organizational structure that feeds our fear. This structure must be challenged by the word of God.

Work is defined as physical or mental activity. The question we must ask ourselves is what are we working with? The substance of things hoped for and the evidence of things not seen, or are we placing hope on what we see? If we are hoping for what we see we will never have peace and forever fool ourselves. Hope again is a feeling that something we desire is possible. The dream killer comes to make us put our confidence in what we see, so we will never use our creative energy to bring into existence what we were created to accomplish. We bring into existence what we chose and the experience of our choice is the reality that we deal with daily. If we tap into this spiritual realm, meditate on our dream and develop mental images for what we desire and work towards bringing it into existence we have just created something with our thoughts. Now we become the spiritual beings that are living out a human experience and in the process reveal the glory of the Lord.

Yet, the danger with meditating and bringing into existence our desires is what we must question: will it glorify the creator, or make us think we are a creator that exists without a divine connection? Fleshy distractions keep us from answering this question, because if we are not in the spirit we will think we are in control of our lives. Some can be so caught up in self that they get to the point where they can care less if the creator is glorified or horrified with their actions. However, in order to get everlasting results out of our lives and to spend fewer days regretting our mistakes, we must reverse the process that causes us to hate our actions. The substance that is hoped for comes from the automatic thoughts that are channeled through suggestions. If the suggestions are negative we must ignore them and be reminded of the fact that whatever we work to bring into existence is what we experience in our lives.

Therefore, we must fight to understand that our choice determines our destiny. Destiny involves daily experiences and how we chalk them up as win or losses. We must not forget that our creator is keeping a score card of our lives and determining if we are wasting or unleashing the creative energy that he has stored up in us. By taking our feeling that something we desire is possible and mixing it with the creative energy that the creator has put inside of us, we bring creative expression into existence. However, if this creative energy is not directed by the spirit of truth we are in danger of experiencing depressive states and anxious moments.

> *In the beginning was the Word, and the Word was with God, and the Word was God.*

John 1:1

Creative expression comes from the words we choose to pay attention to, and if the words were not from the beginning then our creative expression can lead to disappointments, disillusionment, dread and ultimately desperation. However, if we choose to take our creative energy and line it up with the word that was from the beginning there is nothing in hell, heaven or any parts of the earth that will stop all things being possible in our lives. We again must ask ourselves if what we are choosing will allow the automatic thoughts to be negative in our mind. The substance of things hoped for materializes with effort, determination and an aggressive attitude that understands the principles that govern the universe, not wishful thinking.

Our identity is stolen by the working of our flesh. We live in a data-driven society. As a result of this many need to see statistics and projections before decisions are made. We are taught this is an informed decision making practice and if we don't practice this method of thinking we are not being logical. This can establish fear in anyone who steps outside of the data matrix, but this fear controls our destiny. However, if we take the word of the creator and trust his ability, we will find stability in our behaviors and peace that cannot come from the comfort that is provided by researched trends.

In the garden, the serpent asked Eve a question. When she investigated, she self-indulged into nothing and gave her husband some of the forbidden fruit. Just like Adam and Eve, we ask ourselves questions and if we do not respond like Jesus we will get the same results Adam and Eve received; death. The works of the flesh is forbidden fruit that steals our ability to create those things that will bring us everlasting joy and not continued frustration.

Through Adam and Eves' investigation into the forbidden fruit, they transformed a peaceful earth into a chaotic environment. In this chaotic environment the flesh urges us to investigate our *forbidden fruit* which points us in the direction of pleasure instead of realizing a dream that we can treasure.

Adultery is a voluntary work of the flesh between two individuals with one or both of them being unfaithful to their spouse. How can this steal our spiritual identity especially in a world where anything goes? Is this ok? Again if our choices are based on of a society that glamorizes sin than we will never have peace within. This work of the flesh is popular and okay and never takes under consideration the selfish act that only benefits the individual that steps outside of the marriage to fulfill various sexual desires.

> *Having eyes full of adultery and that cannot cease from sin; beguiling unstable souls; a heart they have exercised with covetous practices; cursed children.*

> I Peter 2:14

This is the result of what is created with a fear of "what if?" which can only be answered through our desires. This mindset causes us to not realize that the creator created humanity with a desire and purpose. Once this is misunderstood our identity is stolen and replaced with a fantasy that never develops into a reality. This fantasy is experienced with no stability and false security that develops into a false safety net. This false safety net becomes an addiction that is fueled by fear. How can peace come from this behavior?

What about wedding promises of "We Do?" Self- indulgence into nothing will cause us to forget promises and not be consistent which is not the design or the model that we were created to portray. Once the flesh begins to work, the spirit of truth continues to warn us of the dangerous direction that we are going in. Often the signs are ignored until it is too late. However, if we follow the spirit of truth we will be led to a wonderful experience instead of horrible and traumatizing events.

Trauma comes from a lifestyle of fornication, uncleanness and lasciviousness. If we ever accept the lie and participate in such activities we will experience trauma. If we are truthful to ourselves we will declare it to be an unsatisfying experience. Maybe not in the act itself but the emotional baggage that came as a result of submitting to whatever our flesh suggests. This baggage contains an emotional shock with lasting psychological damage. This damage is the experience that comes with fearful thoughts that arouse the senses. The result is usually a habitual performance that hinders the creative expression that wants to flow daily.

Works of the flesh are very dangerous. These works or events can ultimately affect our behaviors. We become hypnotized by pleasure. According to society's norms, this is considered a successful lifestyle. Once lust has conceived itself, it brings forth death to our destiny because we have rerouted ourselves to committing to social interchange with behavior that we were not created for. This produces a cloudy vision for our life. This unclean mind is stimulated by obscene and indecent behavior birthed by a mindset that everything is "ok". Remember we live in a society that encourages or endorses just about any kind of behavior. This behavior leaves us unbalanced in our thinking. This unbalance is justified by a world that is consumed in lust and uses the five senses as a measuring stick to for success.

> *All things were made by him; and without him was not anything made that was made. In him was life; and the life was the light of men. And the light shines in darkness; and the darkness comprehends it not.*

John 3:4-5

The question that can be asked in this scripture centers around the darkness and that which shines in darkness. In darkness we must focus on the attributes of God and fight to be the light this light within shines through the darkness of this world and enable us to take our dreams to the extreme. This characteristic is the creative expression that can help us to never lose focus on our blessing. This blessing consists of our true identity, which is the creative ability to envision the provision; to lay aside every weight and self-indulgence into nothing that hinders us from our destiny. If we were created in the Lord's image then all things that are made in our life are created by our thinking.

This fact manifests itself into our experiences. The understanding of the process is not grasped because of the psychological effects of unexpected disturbances that leave us unbalanced. It's time for us to dream again and know that the lie is the active agent that the dream killer uses to steal our spiritual identity. This lie produces a lifestyle that is unbalanced and the Bible declares that *a double minded man is unstable in all his ways.* (James 1:8) This instability comes from trying to fit fleshly desires into a spiritual being, but it should be where we allow the spiritual to enlighten our flesh. This will allow us to walk in the spirit of truth.

Truth should not be determined by our senses, but declared by the creative word of God. "*In the beginning was the Word, and the Word was with God, and the Word was God.* "(John 1:1) Only our experiences can confirm the truth of this statement, not a biblical scholar that's influenced by thoughts and opinions, because the truth of our life is manifested into our daily experiences.

CREATIVE ENERGY UNLEASHED

"Be extremely subtle, even to the point of formlessness. Be extremely mysterious, even to the point of soundlessness."

(Art of War)

The thoughts we wrestle with are the ones that are automatic, quick and unknown in purpose so that the intent is not noticed in the suggestion. However, what we experience from our thought process develops into an experience. Our choice determines what that experience will be. This is when creativity comes into existence. What we resist will never exist in our current experience, but the desire that we submit to is the one that will be unleashed and become a part of our daily activities. Too often the choice is not favorable so the outcome is not desirable. This leaves us in a place where we are frustrated and mad at ourselves. We wonder and blunder again and again in a cycle of the same until we either die or get frustrated enough to change. The creative change or remain the same mind-set starts with our thinking. Our decisions impact our vision for our lives. Do we have a vision and if we do is it fragmented with a double mind which leaves us unstable? To allow the creator to create peace in the middle of the chaos, we must submit to a true vision that only comes from the one that created us with a divine purpose.

> *To whom will ye liken me, and make me equal, and compare me that we may be like?*

Isaiah 45:5

We must accept the creator as the solution and not the pollution that has ruined our lives. This is understood through a desperate attitude to become curious about the creative answer that can bring us relief from our daily frustrations over our decision-making process.

Curiosity into the unknown makes the deepest part of our mind bring into reality that which we strongly desire. Unfortunately many of us have the experience of bringing our lust into existence instead of taking our dreams to the extreme. How can what feels, taste, look, sound and smell good be considered so wrong? In determining what is wrong or right do we make our determination from Faith or fear? The choice should be clear by now. How can we walk by faith if we are afraid of what we see?

> *Have not I commanded thee? Be strong and of a good courage; be not afraid, neither be thou dismayed: for the Lord thy God is with thee whithersoever thou goest.*

> Joshua 1:9

Our faith dictates if we will walk with strength and courage in our creator. Or do we walk away from our dream by indulging into nothing. Behavior is acted upon from thoughts that create feelings which inspire us to quit or have the mind of Christ. By having the mind of Christ, we will not make provisions for our flesh. If we make provisions for our flesh we are creating a reality that is distracted by the flesh and never focused on the possibilities that can come from the spirit of truth.

> *The night is far spent, the day is at hand: let us therefore cast off the works of darkness, and let us put on the armour of light. Let us walk honestly, as in the day; not in rioting and drunkenness, not in chambering and wantonness, not in strife and envying. But put ye on the Lord Jesus Christ, and make not provision for the flesh, to fulfill the lusts thereof.*

> Romans 13:12-14

We have spent our lives chasing nothing because we interpret daily events through feelings which dictate our behaviors. We must throw these thoughts out of our mind by being directed by the spirit of truth. As our thoughts create our feelings we must walk honestly before our God so we won't fulfill the lust of the flesh. Once this takes place the creative energy in us is unleashed, and once this event takes place our dreams are released and become a part of our reality. This only occurs when we put on the Lord Jesus Christ and not make provisions for the flesh. In our flesh *"dwells no good thing,"* because it's a trigger for our emotions. These emotions can trick us into believing that we are really chasing our dreams when we are chasing our lust. It's very difficult not to get distracted by the flesh when we are pleasing it with our crazy desires.

First, we must not forget that thoughts create feelings, and the wrong thoughts can create the wrong behavior. What is wrong and right for a person can be argued forever, but to understand if we are unhappy with our life experiences should not be difficult to determine. If we fall in this unhappy category then we need to create some thoughts that are strong enough to override the ones that have been choking our happiness with a bunch of mess. We also must understand the difference between temporal happiness and everlasting happiness; because this is another argument we can use to define our dreams. We must be careful with our source of happiness.

> *But made himself of no reputation, and took upon him the form of a servant, and was made in the likeness of men: And being found in fashion as a man, he humbled himself, and became obedient unto death even the death of the cross.*

> Philippians 2:7-8

The spirit of truth, which is the word of the creator, will guide us down that road where we do not search for a reputation but become a servant. If we allow the spirit of truth to help us understand that in the beginning the spirit of truth came from the creator, and the creator allowed his spirit to become flesh, then this will bless us in knowing that we must die out to the thoughts that cause us so much frustration with our behaviors. The spirit of truth wants us to deny our reputation. This is a difficult task. This will position us to become a servant to man. This positioning can only be done through humility and dying out to selfish desires which will develop into experiences that allow our dreams to be unleashed into a dark world. Our dreams will light our path in the direction for which we were created. Having this understanding we will forever develop feelings that satisfy and not pacify us, which will cause us to abandon our chase of self-indulging into nothing. Again, we must not forget that if we do not want the horror of embarrassing behavior ruining our lives we must put on the armor of light to protect our mind. This protection is needed when we make decisions. If we put on the Lord Jesus Christ we will not make provisions to fulfill the lust of the flesh.

A sign that we are truly allowing our dreams to be taken to the extreme and that our creative energy is being released is the expression of the fruit of spirit becoming a part of our daily behavior.

> *But the fruit of the Spirit is love, joy, peace, longsuffering, gentleness, goodness, faith, Meekness, temperance: against such there is no law. And they that are Christ's have crucified the flesh with the affections and lusts.*

> Galatians 5:23-24

These attributes guarantee life and no more longing to fill the void produced by having unfulfilled dreams. The challenge comes again when trying to distinguish between lust and love for the dream. We must be able to distinguish thoughts from facts in order to realize if we are allowing the dream or the nightmare to become an actuality in our life. The trap or snare is separating thoughts from feelings. We must fight not to see the two as one and cognitive therapists believe that if we distinguish thoughts from facts we can be honest with how we are feeling about our experiences manifested through our behaviors. This procedure helps us come to grips with how our terrible thinking is supported by facts that lead to the behaviors that cause us to be unsatisfied with our life. This is where the fruit of the spirit comes in for anyone that is tired of frustrating behaviors.

The mind of Christ guides us into a lifestyle of love and joy. This behavior is experienced through longsuffering and gentleness which are attributes that must come from thinking with the mind of Christ. How can we produce behavior that is mild and patiently waits and not in a rush all the time? What enables us to ponder on the beneficial part of our life that is filled with confident belief and trust in our dreams? Why should we have thoughts that produce humility and discipline to the point that we have self-restraints in place? These answers come from our experiences that cause us to wonder if we are satisfied or horrified with our daily actions.

Therefore, the facts that come with the thoughts should help us make positive decisions and clear concise choices. We will be satisfied in knowing that we are not chasing after nothing. We will know If we are walking in faith and experiencing the fruit of the spirit in our experiences as we chase our dreams.

Acting in fear can challenge our feelings and behavior because we want to mask the embarrassment and shame and even the frustration of trying to explain a lifestyle of faith. This frustration leads to desperate behavior that often causes many of us to become anxious to find relief for the pain from the hurt that comes after the horrific experience of not acting in faith. Why live a life based on hypotheses, descriptions, and perspectives or guesses? This lifestyle can be avoided when we live a life that's guided by the spirit of truth. This is pointed out by distinguishing thoughts and feelings from facts. An activating event comes when we make decisions that affect our behavior and leave us with consequences that if not guided by the spirit of truth, we are often left frustrated and empty. The change comes when we become frustrated with the consequences that have left us to define our lifestyles in unpleasant ways.

How can the dream change this and what does it have to do with distinguishing facts from feelings and our thoughts?

> *Let no man say when he is tempted, I am tempted of God: for God cannot be tempted with evil, neither tempteth he any man: But every man is tempted, when he is drawn away of his own lust, and enticed. Then when lust hath conceived, it bringeth forth sin: and sin, when it is finished, bringeth forth death.*

> James 1:14-17

The thought which is the creative expression that comes from the creator must not be guided by feelings that are centered on facts that lead to death. It is a no-brainer to identify many behaviors that are very reckless and if continued will lead to the loss of life. However, the dream that God has instilled in everyone can be used to direct us around the pitfalls that come to end our lives. It's just not a natural life but spiritual life that ceases to exist when we self-indulge into nothing. The scripture mentions temptation and many religious people are quick to point to the devil, but the temptation comes from our decision and thought processes as they relate to a desire. In our daily experience for those of us that live by faith the testing of our faith comes with walking by faith. Those that live in fear the desire appears to be a temporary fix to our cravings and fulfillment of our curiosity. In psychological terminology, it's considered an activating event. This is known as a happening which is existing, former, or expected, that prompts irrational ideas and troublesome feelings. These feelings can generate fear or faith that proceed into behaviors and lead to a consequence that is defined as an experience. This experience will come with facts that we have established and created.

However, if we are not drawn away from our dream and stay steadfast and committed to our faith we will not be drawn away by curiosity. This is the category that was mentioned earlier when our lives are lived through hypotheses, descriptions, perspectives and even guesses. The bible declares that this type of thinking will lead to death. This death can be emotional, mental or even physical, and these are big businesses industries in our society.

> *Every good gift and every perfect gift is from above, and cometh down from the father of lights, with whom is no variableness, neither shadow of turning.*

James 1:17

The gift is the creative expression which is produced through our thinking. We must question how we choose to allow ourselves to think about our daily activating events. Do we choose to allow this perfect gift to be directed by our faith or fear? If we will live out the scripture pertaining to James 1:17 and do not deviate from our purpose on planet earth our dreams will go to the extreme. If we were created by the Father of Lights and there is no variableness or shadow of turning in his attributes, why do we allow temptation to distract us from our destiny? To take our dreams to the extreme we must allow the creative energy of the creator to continue to flow through us so that his glory will be revealed. When God's glory is revealed in us then creative energy is unleashed and all flesh shall witness this phenomenal event.

This takes place by being proactive in the spirit and not reactive to the flesh. When we are proactive, we find ourselves meditating on the words of life and not contemplating over the hypotheses, descriptions, and perspectives that often ruin our lives. We must align ourselves with the scripture that instructs us to have the mind of

Christ. When we allow the activating events in our life to be governed by the word of God we can get the results that Jesus received while he was on Earth.

If it's not written in the Word we should not be left somewhere where we are curious over hypotheses, descriptions, and perspectives and even guesses. This often steals our creativity and makes us subject to making provisions for the flesh. If we act in fear from the flesh it will keep us from satisfying the desires that are produced from the fruit of the spirit. When Christ enters our life and we began to walk in the spirit, every day with Jesus is sweeter than the day before. He satisfies with a peace that can never be discovered in this world.

> *O lord thou hast searched me and known me, Thou knowest my downsitting and mine uprising, thou understandest my thought afar off. Thou compassest my paths and my lying down, and art acquainted with all my ways.*

> Psalm 139:1-3

To know that someone knows us to this magnitude is scary. Before the activating event takes place to affect the behavior which will lead us to a consequence. Our creator already knows what our decisions are before we say a yes or no. Where does this leave us? We should be at a point where we are confident in the dream that God has developed in us to take to the extreme. He knows if we doubt what he has placed inside of us or are we disconnecting ourselves from Him. We must not allow our senses to dictate how we view the activating events that will forever be a part of our life. The dream must dictate how we respond to the activating event. Therefore, if the dream is to be unleashed we must trust the one that already knows and is waiting for us to allow his creative ability to flow through us. If we act out the scriptures we will get the God-designed outcome. We must not forget the creator gave us the dream so know it's time to take it to the extreme, by unleashing the creative energy that has been downloaded into our minds. We must not be drawn away from this possibility by curiosity or other factors that want to cause us to be left guessing the outcome.

> "Those who are skilled in combat do not become angered; those who are skilled at winning do not become afraid. Thus the wise win before the fight, while the ignorant fight to win."

> (Tzu, 1988)

The *Art of War* suggests that if we are wise we win before the fight because we have allowed our creative mind to think before we act. When the activating event develops, we know that we are not going to get distracted from our goal. We stay the course and become very bold with our decision-making process. This behavior demonstrates our victorious results over negativity and adds to our happiness with excitement over how we have developed into individuals that are guided by our faith and not fear. Again, our faith produces the result to the vision that came from the dream. This dream was from above which leads and guide us into all truth, but we must remember that the fight is with the desires of our flesh. Our flesh tries to trick us into believing that those desires are the dreams we should be chasing. By doing this we will find our self- indulging into nothing with consequences that are full of frustrating experiences.

PRECISION WITH THE VISION

A skilled attack is one against which opponents do not know how to defend; a skilled defense Is one in which opponents do not know how to attack.

(The Art of War)

There is a vision in every human being that will make provision for the dark days ahead. The vision shows victorious experiences, not disastrous moments in life. These disastrous moments can stem from a false belief that all we do is dream and not work, but the bible declares that faith without works is dead. How do we work toward making the dream that God has instilled within us manifest itself daily?

STEP 1:

The answer is to not allow lustful behavior to attack our possibility to be God's ideal creation. We must not forget that he is the creator. As the Art of War suggests we must attack skillfully so that the dream killer won't know how to defend against our assault. We take the situation and reverse the principle so that we can get the results that we have been denied.

Our thoughts must become aggressive towards obtaining the goal. Aggressive thoughts become passive when fear is used instead of faith. The attack must be towards our lust. We attack lust by trusting God and not our cravings. Lust is an overwhelming craving, which leads to self-indulgence into nothing. The result is death to the dream. A dream is an ambitious aspiration, which must have an overwhelming craving to manifest in our daily experiences. Therefore like the concept that thoughts affect our feelings, the same is how a dream can be guided through an overwhelming craving. It's dangerous to have these ambitious desires centered primarily on physical objectives because what we program our mind with is what will manifest through our behaviors.

STEP 2

It's important to remember that once Christ becomes an active part of our lives failure is over. This is mental step two in taking our dreams to the extreme. We must stay connected to our creative source so our behaviors will give us something to rejoice in. This develops through having ambitious aspirations that are precise with an overwhelming craving. This craving must not be guided by what we see but by what's heavenly downloaded from the creator. We must remember that his words will not return unto him void. If we forgot what his words are, we must fight to remember that God words declared existence out of nothing.

And God said. Let there be light: and there was light.

Genesis 1:3

In the first book of the Bible, the phrase "God said" appears at least nine times. This is why the Bible is viewed as one of the most controversial books in the world. We cannot understand how anyone can speak and what they say comes into existence. We fail to realize that it was not so much the words that were the only part of creation. God thoughts became the creative word. The heaven and earth came into existence in response to His word. As God thoughts are followed through our obedience to his words we develop precision with our vision. Precision is the quality, condition, or fact of being exact and accurate. Once we have faith in God's words and not afraid to trust his words we can be precise with the vision that he has placed in our lives. This vision will create experiences that cannot deny God's glory being manifested through us.

> "When directives are carried out, people are sincerely loyal preparations for defenses are firmly secured, and yet you are so subtle and secretive that you reveal no form, opponents are unsure-their intelligence is of no avail."

(The Art of War, 1988)

We are at war with the dream killer and his weapons are activated through the lust of our flesh. Therefore, we must carry out the creator's directives which are "let it be." As the *Art of War* states, we must be loyal to these directives through meditating and reflecting on how to become better at securing our destinies. This must be secretive through not responding to the suggestions that come through the events that try to activate fear to trust God's word. If we show interest in the fleshly desires we are making provisions for the flesh.

STEP 3

We must exercise patience because the dream killer's intelligence comes from our immediate response to stimuli that develops from fearful responses upon hearing God's creative word. Faith walkers follow these directives and take their dream to the extreme. Consequently, "faith comes by hearing" the message, and the message is heard through Christ. (Romans 10:17)

If we exercise patience during the time of hearing instructions, our creative instincts will produce ideas that will help our dreams become a reality. The fight centers on making a choice to obtain what our soul loves not what our flesh craves. Do we focus on that which lasts or that which ends real fast? Only our experiences can dictate what we define as our reality. We must be truthful in dealing with our pains and hurts. To be precise with our purpose in life we must be honest about where we are right now with this purpose.

STEP 4

A step that must not be forgotten is remembering that we have a spiritual identity that must not be compromised. If this identity is compromised now hurt, pain, frustration and desperation gain a foothold in the mind. Fearful responses are birth from failure to trust God's word.

It's amazing to note that the first part of creation was light. Light is symbolic with understanding. Once an understanding came into existence the rest of creation developed. What does that have to do with our spiritual identity? We are spiritual beings. In order to truly be happy with our decisions and experiences we must act based on the words of the creator. The *creation* was not made from things that were seen.

> *Through faith we understand that the worlds were framed by the word of God, so that things which are seen were not made of things which do appear.*

Hebrews 11:3

We try to create lifestyles based on what we see. This mistake causes our spiritual identity to be compromised. This process always leads to disappointment and lies that cannot even come close to promises that were guaranteed. However, if we center our mind on a *must have* attitude we will always acquire the desire. This desire is the motivating factor in our mind. Precision on the vision is centered on faith in the objective and realizing that we are not going to see what we want until we envision what we want. If we are happy or unhappy depends on if the soul agrees to our outcome. Also, the things that we see were created by someone that had a desire that bloomed into action which manifests itself into what is now in existence. The question is will we use this principle with precision and fight to manifest our vision?

STEP 5

"The subtle is stillness, the mysterious is movement. Stillness is defense, movement attack."

(The Art of War, 1988)

Subtle is defined as being perceptive. Stillness comes when waiting on the Lord. Our defense is based on how we use our faith while we wait. We use our faith to attack the fear that is trying to make our vision unclear.

But those who hope in the LORD will renew their strength. They will soar on wings like eagles; they will run and not grow weary, they will walk and not be faint.

(Isaiah 40:31)

For the dream to be taken to the extreme we must be accurate with our actions, and walk in the spirit and not the flesh. The fruits of the spirit can manifest in our actions and guarantee us outcomes that make us proud. Temperance is a fruit of the spirit that is related to being subtle and stillness is being patient which is mysterious. Stillness requires patience. Being patient is not always easy. However in James 1:3, the bible tells us *"the trying of our faith worketh patience."*

Again, faith is not what is seen but is established on our hope. This is mysterious in its movement because it cannot be seen by the natural eye. Therefore patience is our defense because we are waiting on the creator to manifest his promise through his words "Let there be." The mind is warring with remembering that the light in the beginning was the first part of creation. When we understand what our weapons are, we conqueror the fears that always war against our faith.

For though we walk in the flesh, we do not war after the flesh: For the weapons of our warfare are not carnal, but mighty through God to the pulling down of strong holds; Casting down imaginations, and every high thing that exalteth itself against the knowledge of God, and bringing into captivity every thought to the obedience of Christ.

II Corinthians 10:3-5

The war is not based on what we see, but on the strong holds that cause us to be caught up in our imaginations. These imaginations fuel our fear. The strong holds that hinder our progress and produce chaos in our lives are built in our imagination, but there is a creative word that can cast down these imaginations. Remember that the mind of Christ centers on humility and the opposite of this mind set are vain or high imaginations. However, once we allow the creative word to be precise in our life we bring these imaginations into the obedience to Christ. The important point to remember is that the fleshly desires that feed our imagination must be attacked by the word of God. If this attack is not executed our flesh will be fed by an imagination that creates desires and ideas that are contrary to God's plan for our lives. We must be precise with the vision that produces experiences that validate our reality (failure or victorious living) in our lives. We must move with precision staying focused on our vision and remain still keeping our movements mysterious.

STEP 6

"The individual without strategy who takes opponents lightly will inevitably become the captive of others."

(The Art Of War, 1988)

It's a sad fact that many take the war in the mind lightly. Therefore we must be very aggressive in our fight against fleshy desires. If we take this war lightly we will be held captive by imaginations that exalt themselves above God. Therefore we must be precise with the fight. These imaginations can trick us into lusting after nothing instead of trusting in the word of God. It would be very unfortunate if a person spent their entire life held captive by desires that resulted in their ruin. The experiences speak for themselves and come with many unbearable consequences. These resulting consequences and their effects on the human mind have created a lucrative business in the area of mental health care.

STEP 7

"If you have no ulterior scheme and no forethought, but just rely on your individual bravery, flippantly taking opponents lightly and giving no consideration to the situation, you will surely be taken prisoner."

(Art of War, 1988)

A prisoner is a hostage. This is how many of us see ourselves when fighting depression and anxiety. Fear stimulates the imagination reminding us of the desire that is holding us hostage. These temporary pleasures keep us in bondage. After the behavior is carried out, the cycle of longing again for something stronger develops into anxiety or depression. However, Christ has come to break the chains that have been wrapped around our brains, and turned on the light of understanding into our destiny. Once this purpose is discovered then we must allow the Lord to cause us to be precise on his will. Therefore, this strategy must be carried out by thinking with the mind of Christ not with the mind of what pleasures can eliminate our pain for a small season.

> *Finally, brethren, whatsoever things are true, whatsoever things are honest, whatsoever things are just, whatsoever things are pure, whatsoever things are lovely, whatsoever things are of good report; if there be any virtue, and if there be any praise, think on these things.*

Philippians 4:8

FAITH

Open thou mine eyes, that I may behold wondrous things out of thou law.

Psalm 119:18

"Skilled users of arms first cultivate the way that makes them invincible, keep their rules, and do not miss defeatist confusion in opponents."

(Tzu, 1988)

Faith and fear is based on a law and order based off of the choice. We must determine how anxious are we to take our dreams to the extreme by remembering the law and rules that govern success of the unseen. This law must be activated by the desire that is stimulated by a strong desire to take our everlasting dreams to the extreme. Let's look at this through a simple four step process: we think, believe, act and receive a reward or punishment.

Is faith or fear the motivating factor behind the thoughts that are causing us to act? The consequence of the action reinforces the behavior which produces a cycle of madness or the glory of the Lord being revealed in us. We must be honest enough to ask ourselves does this idea produce everlasting happiness in our lives? If we say we are happy then we must ask ourselves how long does this happiness last? If the happiness ends quickly then we must question our belief system that does not produce an experience of everlasting joy. Unfortunately, we live in a world where everything is fast and the definition of success is based on what is seen.

An acronym we can use to help us understand faith is **F**ocusing **A**lways on **I**nner spiritual **T**houghts that will forever make us **H**appy. The dictionary describes faith as complete trust or confidence in someone or something. As we develop confidence in people we believe their words and reputation to be something that can make us invincible to our problems. (Art of War) In the confidence game this is called manipulation. The con artist's goal is to gain our trust so we'll believe the lie. Again, as we seek out for that plan that can make us conquer our fears of gaining success we must question our thoughts. Are we having trust and confidence in a lie or the creative word?

> *Now faith is the substance of things hoped for, the evidence of things not seen.*

Hebrews 11:1

Are we allowing the substance that we hoped for to be controlled by fear? Do we rely on evidence that is not seen or what is seen? As ideas come to our minds we act with the mind-set that we will be happy, with the decisions that we make. However, the consequences that accompany our behaviors through reward or punishment reinforce the truth or the lie with this statement. The challenge is surrendering to or accepting thoughts that will always make us happy. We are even challenged by the concept of happiness because we think what we see makes us happy. Sometimes it can but most of the time it's a trick of mind to get us to believe a lie. How often have we been deceived by what we see?

The definition of happiness to many is varied with various beliefs. Yet, depression accompanies some of these beliefs and if not depression a state of anxiety. The question should be how we accept thoughts that will forever make us happy enough to be free of stressful anxiety.

Happiness has two definitions: the worlds and the creative words. Which definition do we use to experience our happiness? The definition we use dictates whether we are going to exercise faith or fear in our decision making process. Often, we blame others for the mistakes that we have made. We have to suffer the consequence of our decisions, or we become happy with reaping the benefits of our decisions. The wisdom of this statement is allowing ourselves to have faith in God. This thinking centers on the ability to exercise faith over fear. Happiness is sometimes compromised by being tricked by what we think will make us happy. *The Art of War* suggests that we become skilled users of arming our thoughts by cultivating the mind in a way that makes our thinking invincible to fear. If we become consistent in keeping these rules, we are actively replacing fear with faith. By committing to this process we never miss an opportunity to defeat confusion. We have to be able to fight the thoughts that want to exalt themselves above God. We must fight the good fight of faith and take our dreams to the extreme by knowing that the creative energy that God has put in us will lead us to true happiness.

We must make the commitment to focus on the inner thoughts that produce true happiness. This commitment must be met daily in order to take our dream to the extreme consistently. This will reveal the glory of the Lord.

We must believe that without faith it's impossible to please God. As the glory of the Lord is revealed in our lives we constantly desire his presence to be the creative energy that is used to help establish the vision we need to see us through our daily challenges. This helps us fight the distractions that want us to trust in what we see, and not who God want us to be. If we allow this process to flow, we will be desperate for God's creative presence daily. This will fuel the necessary motivation to consistently change, and the bible declares this as being not conformed to this world but being transformed by the renewing of our mind. With this mindset we will not hide our thoughts and intentions. We will hate that which is evil and adhere to that which is good because we analyze the actions that lead to unhappiness.

When we analyze our actions, we cannot be in denial concerning our thoughts that produced the unhappy experience. Remember our first thoughts were this unhappy consequence which was triggered by our thinking. We made a decision with hopes that we were going to be happy. Again we must be careful about our motivation, is it by fear or faith? This is developed through being truthful about our choices and knowing that the results of that which is evil subtracts from our happiness and kills our joy. If our happiness and joy is frozen so is our motivation to forget, reach and press towards our future ambitions. Depression comes from hopelessness, but allowing the spirit of truth to guide us through faith we discover how to stay free of this monster.

> *Not slothful in business; fervent in spirit; serving the Lord: Rejoicing*
> *in hope; patient in tribulation; continuing instant in prayer.*

> Romans 12:11-12

This scripture directs us to the last part of the acronym of faith. The letter "**i**" in faith should represent inner motivation from the mind. The letter "**t**" is thoughts. The letter "**h**" is happiness from the decisions that we make daily. Inner is focusing on what's within and not that which is on the outside. The inside of us is the soul. The soul is the seat of our emotions. Trusting what is within can be tricky because we are always challenged with our inner lust. This mindset of trusting should not be slothful in business. These spiritual thoughts will lead us down the road to happiness because our actions are not ruled or control by our five senses. These five senses truly work to inform us of the world around us but not by the world that our dreams can create as a reality. This reality can unquestionably create our everlasting happiness. Once our mind rejoices in hope and become patient in tribulation and continues in prayer, we will not suffer from the depression epidemic. Fervent is being enthusiastic and passionate with the confidence that the prayers of the righteous avail.

> "It is swift as the wind in that it comes without a trace and withdraws
> like lightning it is like a forest in that it is orderly. It is rapacious a fire
> across a plain, not leaving a single blade of grass. It is immovable as a
> mountain when it garrisons."

> (Tzu, 1988)

The answer to our prayers is as swift as the wind, because in the decision process if we use faith and not fear we operate based on the same method that was used during the creation of the world. Therefore, we can use our faith to move the unmovable mountains in life. This mindset will arm us when we fight our fear which tries to attack our mind. If we are instant in prayer our answer to hopelessness will come swift like the wind. This answer will rescue us from misery and place a smile on our face. The solution to the problem will not withdraw but come like lightning, but be so orderly to bring us happiness with a greedy fire that is determined to burn out all thoughts of sadness and despair. The creator is determined to prove to us that he cares about our success and wants to bring us eternal happiness. His promise is like an immovable mountain, which is stationary and fixed on accomplishing his word. God's word went out and will not return unto him void. His words fill the void and will not leave us in a state of despair and anxiety.

Therefore, in order to be free of depression we must have faith in God the creator. This must be the motivation that does not come by works but through the creative energy that produces positive results. This is a direct result from trusting the creator.

Faith is not confusion but is a guide that will lead us into all truth. The truth directs us on how to act when various lusts want to draw us away from trusting in the dream of being free of depression. We must never lose our confidence in this reconnection with the creator, because it will help us implement the dream that the creator has sent. Our desire to accomplish the dream develops into confidence with the faith that produces the courage to implement the thoughts that must develop into behaviors. Then we can be happy with the results that come from our dream being taking to the extreme. This helps us have the mind of Christ and work to finish the work that he gave us to do through being enthusiastic with the creative energy that feeds our ideas. We must be careful not to allow negativity to poison our choices.

> *Treasures of wickedness profit nothing: but righteousness delivereth from death. The Lord will not suffer the soul of the righteous to famish: but casteth away the substance of the wicked.*

(Proverbs 10:2-3)

The idea of something being lost or the experience of losing and gaining with the knowledge that the cycle constantly repeats itself produces a lot of anxiety. However, having confidence in the fact that the righteousness that comes by being led by the spirit will not allow the dream to die is very encouraging. This encouragement is the faith that is necessary to fight off all the negative aggression that tries to lead us away from the creator. The creator produces our happiness and joy that will never cease.

The question for many is what thoughts are we implementing in our actions fear or faith? How do we execute and bring into realization the plans that will guarantee our happiness? Tears often come when we think about our past failures and painful losses. We must be convinced that failure is over and not listen to the whispers from the past. Also, we should have confidence in the creator because his plan is not a plan to fail. If we are not directed by God plans, we our guided by plans that are designed to fail and not secure our happiness. We might get the woman, job, big house or whatever but when we sit back the longing is still there. Our soul is crying for something that we just cannot figure out. We don't understand the longing because our natural man has acquired much status in this world. Yet, there is another world that is crying for attention, and that's the spiritual realm that produces peace that only comes from the prince of peace.

This lack of peace is why millionaires often kill themselves or famous actors or sport figures are caught up in actions that create the next crazy news headline. In order for tragedy not to follow the rich and famous happiness must be centered on the God given dream. Again how do we execute and bring into realization this peace that will guarantee that this void can be filled and grant us everlasting joy? Remember this joy comes with a peace that a poor man can be excited and delighted about because he has discovered something that is far better than a piece of bread. This joy can erase suicidal tendencies that might have followed us all our lives. This joy can be the song that brings peace to us in the middle of a lonely night. This joy is the fabric that holds the dream together with much enthusiasm and excitement to know that the next day and the future is something to look forward to and not something to be run away from. However, the question remains how can this be an active part of our lives?

So then faith cometh by hearing and hearing by the word of God.

Romans 10:17

This scripture instructs us to pay close attention to what we hear. Everyone might not believe that faith comes from simply hearing the word of God. However, we must hear from the creator of the dream if we are going to take that dream to the extreme. The implementation of the dream comes through hearing and by being obedient to what the creator has said in his word.

Firm in defense, victorious in offense, able to keep whole without ever losing, seeing victory before it happens, accurately recognizing defeat before it occurs this is called truly subtle penetration of mysteries.

(Art of War)

Complete confidence in God establishes a solid foundation in the mind. Used offensively, faith gives us the victory because it helps us maintain our focus. It gives us the confidence in the words that return to the creator with positive results, not false promises. Remember positive things add to our lives and negative things subtract. Having our confidence in words that will bring positive results guarantee a life of happiness. Faith sees victory before it happens and accurately recognizes defeat. We must be led by the spirit of truth. In understanding the art of war, faith is known as a penetrator of mysteries, because having confidence in the unseen is a huge mystery. Yet, the results lead us away from the depression epidemic. It's not based on what is seen but what's not seen.

The creator needs a tool to allow his glory to be revealed and this is how the dream can be implemented in our lives. We are either used or abused in life. Our choices determine which one it will be; abused by the world's systems or being used by the master. Therefore, having a mind to act or not react will help us as we are attacked by doubt, hesitation, uncertainty or disbelief.

"Attack complete emptiness with complete fullness,"

(Art of War, 1988)

When we attack we must be empty of our desire and full of the creator's desire. This will grant us results that we are not accustomed to. Remember in order to get different results we must do something different. Instead of acting in our strength we must act in the strength of the master who will lead us out of disaster, because victory is obtainable. Whatever we want badly enough is what will become an active part of our lives. Our experiences are the evidence that proves this point. The next time our lust tries to draw us away from our dream let's attack these strong desires by becoming empty of ourselves and full of the creator's desire for a successful outcome. This outcome involves staying focused on his plan for our success. We must remember that we are the tools that the creator wants to use for his glory to be revealed for all flesh to see. We can show that we have the victory over our various lustful behaviors. This is the direct result of us taking our dreams to the extreme in our lives. Also we cannot be afraid to put complete trust in God and not in our fears in order for this reality to be experienced.

> *Every valley shall be exalted, and every mountain and hill shall be made low: and the crooked shall be made straight, and the rough places plain: And the glory of the Lord shall be revealed, and all flesh shall see it together: for the mouth of the Lord hath spoken it.*

Isaiah 40:4-5

FAILURE IS NOT AN OPTION

"The multitudes know when you win, but they do not know that it is based on the formations of the enemy. They know the traces of attainment of victory, but do not know the abstract form that makes for victory."

(Art of War, 1988)

Victory is a successful conquest and triumph over the enemy. A win that will never end should be everyone's desire. The fight not to fall and the desire to achieve what we believe makes us a winner. It is important to know that we are successful in reaching objectives even if it's being depressed because we were successful in continuing a behavior that led to depression. Again, that which we put in our minds to do, can guarantee us the fact that we will accomplish the goal. Once we desire whatever it is we go after it and don't stop until we obtain it. Our desire fuels the mentality we need to develop for the fight. To remain sane in the midst of much confusion we must remember that no weapon formed against us shall prosper. Therefore, fear is used as a weapon to intimidate us and having this understanding teaches that the same lustful fire can carry us to victory. The victory is not gained by power nor by might but by the Lord's spirit. Remember this spirit will lead and guide us into all truth and the truth is that we were created not to lose, but it's based on what we choose. The question we ask ourselves in the battle is what are we choosing fear or faith? Fear to cause us to fear the lust and surrender to its desires or faith to redirect our actions to fight with confidence in the word of God.

Although it was mentioned that we are not designed to fail let's get a clear understanding of failure. Failure is a breakdown or stoppage that includes disappointment. We must understand that this breakdown and stoppage develops through a choice that we have successfully agreed to and are now receiving the results from. Although this accomplishment is disappointment through the pain of the experience we understand that yes we have mess but the choice was a success. Crazy as it sounds and as real as the letdown and catastrophe is, we must take this failure and reverse the process. We will then find success that guarantees happiness. Therefore, our choice produced results or outcomes. Although the outcome might not have been what we were expecting we did receive an outcome. This outcome did not fail to give us a reality check. The experience will help us understand if we are on the right road or traveling down the wrong path.

> *Ho, everyone that thirsteth, come ye to the waters, and he that hath no money; come ye, buy, and eat; yea, come, buy wine and milk without money and without price. Wherefore do ye spend money for that which is not bread? And your labour for that which satisfeth not? Hearken diligently unto me, and eat ye that which is good, and let your soul delight itself in fatness. Incline your ear, and come unto me; hear, and your soul shall live; and I will make an everlasting covenant with you, even the sure mercies of David.*

Isaiah 55:1-3

The answers to our questions lies in our choices. When we are thirsty do we seek the waters that will cause us to never thirst again, or are we being pacified with lies? Our choices will produce happiness or sadness. The automatic thoughts often sneak up on us, but we cannot afford to behave like we have in the past. We must remember that we want our happiness to last.

If we don't take a moment and slow down to think in terms of the end result we will continue the circle of sadness. Instead of making a judgment by allowing our feelings to dictate our outcome, we must slow down and listen for the guidance of the Holy Spirit. Again, in the moment when we must make a choice we must understand that we are positioned to turn our happiness on or turn it off. Making judgments influenced by the opinions of others is very dangerous because it's our happiness that's at stake.

Grandma used to say, "Haste make waste" so let's not be quick to act, but let's lend our ear to God, be still and see the salvation of the Lord.

An automatic thought is quick which comes from fear or faith and works as an element of surprise. Before we know it, we are being dragged back down the road of despair and confusion which causes us to doubt our very existence on planet Earth. In moments like these we are not even thinking about the promises of God. Illogical thought patterns disrupt our creative energy and instead of being a success we are a living mess. We must fight not to become subject to negativity because failure is not an option. Failure is success turned upside down. We just have to turn failure right side up to win. It takes more than words to get the job done. Acting with spiritual logic and not randomly behaving from impulses will bring joyful results.

Therefore, we must resist being complacent toward options that are not designed to be a part of our existence. This is a daily fight. We were not created to fail, and we must not be content with a life that is consistent where our dream doesn't become a reality. The pressure from the past and the strong urge to conform to the stimuli that draws us from God must be consistently viewed as unrealistic. This is not an option. When thoughts are formed from past experiences we must apply the word of God. We must recognize that entertaining these thoughts are not a choice to relieve tension. Failure to recognize the creator as the tension solution will only add problems to our lives.

The pressure from the temptation needs an outlet. We often use our impulses to direct us into a recycling process where we fall for the bait which causes us to participate in the action that eliminate the true foundation of our happiness. Yes, the release of the tension is temporary fulfillment but when the consequences for the actions are experienced we realize we need deliverance from the negative crave that have made us a slave. The cycle of failure which produces a desire, crave, ache, hunger and attitude that we want it very much must be directed towards our dreams.

> *Seek ye the Lord while he may be found, call ye upon him while he is near: Let the wicked forsake his way, and the unrighteous man his thoughts: and let him return unto the Lord, and he will have mercy upon him: and to our God, for he will abundantly pardon. For my thoughts are not your thoughts, neither, are your ways my ways, saith the Lord.*

Isaiah 55:6-8

The key is to seek the Lord, forsake our ways and return to the Lord. Why should we take such an active approach toward the Lord? For what do we need to be pardoned of? How can we value the importance of the creator's thoughts?

Honesty is the solution for our mental pollution. Theories, opinions, arguments and other vocal statements have poisoned our mind and hindered us from allowing our dreams to become a reality. We should take an active approach towards the Lord. This action seeks the happiness that does not end with disaster, and does not give us moments of exhilaration followed by frustration. We must not be satisfied with hours of cheers followed by tears of agony. We must understand that failure to be happy is not an option.

There is a creator that has not stopped creating a happy ever after, and this is not a fairy tale. If this is an experience we desire, then we must resist negative impulses. We can explain negative in simple math terms. If it subtracts from our happiness it's a negative automatic thought that habitually causes frustration. Yes, it's masked in beauty with bells and whistles but we must be strong in the Lord and the power of his might. This active approach helps us to get a pardon from this self-indulgence into nothing. This comes with distraction from old habits that cause us to forget about taking our spiritual dreams to the extreme. If it's a spiritual dream connected to the creator, then our thoughts are not like the thoughts of those that are around us, and this should encourage us not to get tripped up by their words. If we measure our success like the world measure success, we will always be a state of mental chaos. If we are honest, we know that our experience with chasing what has been suggested to us by others has led to many frustrating days.

For as the rain cometh down and the snow from the heaven, and returneth not thither, but waterth the earth, and maketh it bring forth and bud, that it may give seed to the sower, abnd bread to the eater. So shall my word be that goeth forth out of my mouth: it shall not return unto me void but it shall accomplish that which I please, and it shall prosper in the thing whereto I sent it.

(Isaiah 55:11-12)

The opposite of fear is faith. In order not to be disappointed with the choices we make we must not allow ourselves to continue in a cycle of fear. It has been said if we keep doing the same thing expecting different results than madness will never be replaced with gladness. Mental illness is the quiet epidemic that has affected many to the point that it's not recognized until a tragedy takes place. However, if we trust the creative word we have no cause to fear its' results. The creator guarantees that the creative word will not return to him without taking our dream to the extreme. We will be successful in freeing ourselves of the tension that builds up and seeks a release. The bible declares that we should cast our care upon him for he cares for us. Once this is done then we will be in a position to experience the happiness that produces a peaceful lifestyle. The only way this can be done is if we forsake our thoughts and return unto the Lord. Remember this has to be actively done, not passively considered. We must act with urgency because there are impulses within us with the objective of stealing our joy yet, our choice will determine if we smile with happiness or sigh with temporary pleasure that is good to the flesh and devastating to our destiny.

Will we accept the creator's words that create a solution or are we caught up with negative words that develop negative pollution in our minds? The bible instructs us to be not conformed to this world but be transformed by the renewing of our minds. Let us transform our fear into faith. This is how we replace this negative mindset. This is the process of having the ability to not conform to this world and conform to the mind of Christ. The evidence is the scriptures that contradict the negative thoughts which produce the peace of God that passes all of our understanding.

And the peace of God, which passeth all understanding, shall keep your minds through Christ Jesus.

Philippians 4:7

This is what's needed to fight the negativity that tries to subtract from our happiness while we are chasing our spiritual dreams. To dispute the arguments that contradict the negative thoughts we have to think of some productive strategies. These strategies are active procedures that we take against cognitive distortions that change the direction of our destiny. This is why we must have the mindset that failure is not an option. We are going somewhere but must decide on where we end up, because we are moving in the spirit or the flesh. In order to not believe the desires of the flesh the procedures we must follow are first to incline our ear and draw nigh to the creator. Once we draw nigh to him he draws nigh to us. Now we will understand that our dream will live with happiness and the peace of God. This is a promise that guarantees never to be erased. The void that is present in every human becomes filled when we allow the holy- spirit to come into our life to deny negative thinking. *"Incline your ear, and come unto me; hear, and your soul shall live; and I will make an everlasting covenant with you even the sure mercies of David." (Isaiah 55:3).* This is how happiness is pursued with a suggestion that is enticing, Once the suggestion is followed we are either satisfied or disappointed. If we follow the instructions of the Lord we are truly satisfied because there is a peace that passes our understanding but satisfies with an everlasting promise that we can have forever. A sad part of human existence is receiving a reward with joy and happiness but eventually that happiness wears thin and we reach for something else again and again. However, the holy-spirit is a guide that leads us into all truth. Once we keep being led by the spirit and not the flesh the peace of God is what adds to our happiness. The amazing fact about this peace is that it does not disappear in the time of trouble yes we will feel the pain and frustration in the most trying moments in life, but this is where the peace of God meets us and help us through these moments. Unfortunately, this cannot be brought in the store or discovered through a positive self-help book. Repentance of our self-indulgence into nothing is the key to failure not being an option in our life.

> *But made himself of no reputation, and took upon him the form of a servant, and was made in the likeness of men: And being found in fashion as a man, he humbled himself, and became obedient unto death, even the death of the cross. Wherefore God hath highly exalted him and given him a name which is above every name.*

> Philippians 2:7-9

This is the mind that is suggested by the Apostle Paul in the Bible that is the evidence that should support our thoughts. A mind that seeks not for a reputation, but is in the form of a servant which serves the spiritual desires that comes straight from the true and living God. This mind is humble and becomes obedient unto death which will help us to fight negative filters and not act off of emotional reasoning. God will exalt us over the situations that want to drag us down to the level where we live a life that is filled with cognitive distortions. These cognitive distortions cause us to reject any evidence that contradict negative thoughts, but all praise goes to God because his word will not return unto him void. His words in the beginning up until now are "let there be" and this becomes the spring board for our dreams being taken to the extreme.

Again he said unto me, Prophesy upon these bones, and say unto them O ye dry bones, hear the word of the Lord. Thus saith the Lord God unto these bones; behold, I will cause breath to enter into you and ye shall live. And I will lay sinews upon you, and will bring up flesh upon you, and cover you with skin, and put breath in you, and ye shall live; and ye shall know that I am the Lord

Ezekiel 37:5-6

This scripture presents God's promise for the restoration of Israel. The promise is given in an awesome vision experienced by Ezekiel. God's promise to Israel, given so many years ago, is still valid. The promise for today is failure is not an option. Once we allow the Holy Spirit to carry us we will have a vision as powerful. We will know that the vision has directions leading of the peace and happiness that result from our dreams becoming a reality. These prophesies contained scriptures that reveal how the Lord wants to take our creative expressions and connect them to his word. Once we allow the creator's words to breathe into our dreams they will live and go to the extreme. After this incredible manifestation, we will know that God is the creator he says he is. He is the one that can create the peace to keep us stable in an unstable world that does not want our creativity to live.

For my thoughts are not your thoughts, neither are your ways my ways, saith the Lord. For as the heavens are higher than the earth, so are my ways higher than your ways, and my thoughts than your thoughts. For as the rain cometh down, and the snow from heaven, and returneth not thither, but watereth the earth, and maketh it bring forth and bud, that it may give seed to the sower, and bread to the eater: So shall my word be that goeth forth out of my mouth: it shall not return unto me void, but it shall accomplish that which I please, and it shall prosper in the thing whereto I sent it. For ye shall go out with joy and be led forth with peace: the mountains and the hills shall break forth before you into singing, and all the trees of the filed shall clap their hands. Instead of the thorn shall come up the fir tree, and instead of the brier shall come up the myrtle tree: and it shall be to the Lord for a name, for an everlasting sign that shall not be cut off."

Isiah 55:8-13

God's thoughts are potent and able to free us from the captivity of the fear that causes us to pause when it comes to our destiny. We must remember that it's neither by power nor might but by trusting God's spirit that we reach our destiny. The Lord's words are creative in their intent. This guarantees the results we hope for, so failure in our life is no longer an option.

EXISTENCE SHOULD NOT END IN DEATH

The ungodly are not so: but are like the chaff which the wind driveth away. Therefore the ungodly shall not stand in the judgement, nor sinners in the congregation of the righteous. For the Lord knoweth the way of the righteous: but the way of the ungodly shall perish

Psalms 1

We must have the mind that refuses to entertain the temptation to repeat past negative behaviors. Emotions may flood our thoughts, but we cannot allow them to steal our joy or cause us to act in response to automatic thoughts. We need spiritual assistance when we are pressed by these desire-driven thoughts. This is the moment when of our desires are about to be poured into the object of our yearning. As our mind process this time and opportunity, we must realize that if not led by the spirit, the flesh will automatically remind us of our allegiance. At this point disloyalty comes in the wave of being disobedient to whatever tries to hinder us from reaching our lustful goal. However, what if this process is reversed what will be our outcome? If the outpouring through the stimuli can be the trigger to get us to become disloyal to the desire that kills our spiritual dreams, what would be the experience? How badly do we want to reverse the process of our faith over fear? Do we want to try something different instead of the same old pleasure that eventually gets stale? We should question why we continue to let the chaos prevail? However, our desire should change to letting the urge for the negative and the strong will for the routine to be replaced with the motivation to keep our dreams alive. This is when we must prophesy to a will that is inactive and a desire that's motionless. For the dream to be taken to the extreme we must not let past strong desires cause us to get unfocused on our goal. If the past desire distracts us at the wrong time, then it will slowly destroy how God wants to use us. The dream must live and not die if we intend to have joy and never-ending happiness Now that we are born again and the old man is dead, we must be determined to not allow our lustful behaviors to kill our dreams.

To live as the Lord want us is to understand that this is to exist and survive the negative urges. We must understand that there is a spiritual hierarchy of needs that are indirect conflict with needs of the flesh. The desire to experience our spiritual needs being met must replace the old experiences of the flesh needs being met. This is the challenge that the Christian faces every day.

Our mentality should be like David's when he stated, *"I shall not die, but live and declare the works of the Lord."* (Psalm 119:17) This mentality will take us through the intense moments which spark our desire to adhere to our spiritual hierarchy of needs. Once we reconnect to our purpose our direction in life becomes clear. This helps us recognize the distractions that try to kill this purpose. Our purpose must live, if not we won't be in position to declare the works of the Lord. The works of the Lord develop the outcomes that grant us peace and happiness.

The fight is with our negative thoughts that remind us of past experiences. However, we must make a choice; do we want these experiences to live or our dream to be taken to the extreme? We must never forget that our choices determine our reality. Changed behavior comes from changed thoughts which produce changed behavior. Alternatives must be fought for and not argued against if we know that happiness is a void that is sought after daily in our lives. As Christians, there are thoughts that are stimulated through our senses, and remind us of our past. The past fights our dream, which develops the actions for our behaviors. What alternatives are better for us?

> *Not as though I had already attained, either were already perfect: but I follow after, if that I may apprehend that for which also I am apprehended of Christ Jesus. Brethren, I count not myself to have apprehended: but this one thing I do, forgetting those things which are behind and reaching forth unto those things which are before, I press toward the mark for the prize of the high calling of God in Christ Jesus.*

Philippians 3:12-13

As Christians, we cannot accept the feeling that we have already reached a level of perfection. Paul also mentions in I Corinthians 15:35 the principle of a seed dying brings life. The seed of destruction births fear and must not be accepted. We must accept thoughts from the creator. We must die out to the will of our flesh and live in Christ through the spirit. Once this happens we are quickened with the spirit of expectation. The change in behavior is dependent upon how we take upon the attitude that we have not yet gained the main prize. We are still in a mental fight to allow God's presence to rule our lives. Once his presence is in charge we are moving in the direction of forgetting those things which are behind and reaching forth unto those things which are before and pressing towards the mark of the prize of the high calling which is in Christ Jesus. What is this prize of the high calling? The prize of the high calling is the realization that our dreams can be taken to the extreme. As we move up the spiritual hierarchy of needs we reconnect to our purpose. Once we reconnect to our purpose and walk in the spirit the desire to reach the prize of the high calling replaces the desire to satisfy the flesh. There will always be an impulsive wave to obey the negative crave, but we cannot be hesitant about forgetting those things which are behind us. This is the alternative which is forgetting the past and reaching forth towards the future. This process must become an active part of our lives. If we are not careful the desires produced through automatic thoughts can hinder us in reaching the prize of the high calling. Therefore, our desire to forget reach and press must be stronger than our past desires of wobbling around in past mess. The experience of the past must be fought with a desire to press toward the mark of the prize of the high calling which is in Christ Jesus. Remember he is the Prince of Peace, and this is what we want to be unleashed in our lives. The prince of peace guarantees ultimate happiness.

Once these spiritual needs are met then we must seek to identify with Christ's success. Christ was successful because he surrendered to the will of his father. The will of his father was the spiritual dream that was downloaded from heaven. Christ was not distracted by the world system. The world system was determined to cause Christ to adjust to their worldly objectives. We must acknowledge the principles of Christ and make them a part of our lifestyle. This will automatically isolate the fleshly intent from our mentality. This will help us discover a perfect peace that surpasses our understanding.

Identifying with Christ's success is exercising an alternative option in our lives this is an active mental process to replace the fear that plagues us. Fear causes us to panic and become apprehensive with the move that God wants to perform in our lives. We often worry about what others are going to say about our new behavior and hesitant in allowing the past to die. In order for life to take place, death must come to that which lived before. This is the example that comes from Christ. Christ died that we might live and live more abundantly.

> *The thief cometh not, but for to steal, and to kill and to destroy: I am come that they might have life, and that they might have it more abundantly.*

> John 10:10

Abundantly is defined as the intent to give us a mind of large quantities and an action that is plentiful. Our actions that produce abundant living for us develop from intentions that come from thoughts that constantly fight negative stimuli. Therefore, we must not forget that as we dream about our future endeavors there is a thief that comes to steal, kill and destroy. The thief's objective is to steal our ideas that produce positive behavior. Once the thief has run away with the idea, the next objective is to kill the hope that wonderful expectations will be realized in our lives. If the hope is erased, depression and the accompanying negative behaviors occur. To combat this, we must not be afraid to embrace Christ. He came that we might have an abundant stress free life. It's difficult to let go of things that have a past intimate association with. However we must release these things so they are no longer able to deceive us. The fight to release the past is one we must win repeatedly.

We cannot afford to allow fear to reside in our self-image. Doing so will rob us of the unconditional love that the creator has designed for us to experience. Again these experiences create memories that are the negative darts that attack us but can only be defeated by the shield of faith. This faith is the confidence we have in the creator of our happiness.

> *Wherefore take unto you the whole armor of God that ye may be able to withstand in the evil day, and having done all to stand. Stand therefore, having your loins girt about with truth, and having on the breastplate of righteousness; And your feet shod with the preparation of the gospel of peace; Above all, taking the shield of faith, wherewith ye shall be able to quench all the fiery darts of the wicked. And take the helmet of salvation, and the sword of the spirit, which is the word of God.*

> Ephesians 6:13-16

The "evil day" is any time our faith is challenged by fear. To be successful in that day we must put on the whole armor of God. Yes, there are many ways to distance ourselves from the past. If we decide that we don't want our existence to end in death, then we must stand in faith and not fear. The trial of our faith can be intense because of the automatic thoughts that remind us of our past. Remember that the scripture encourages us above all to take the shield of faith which can quench all the fiery darts. The automatic thoughts are the fiery darts that our faith protects us from as we embrace a future that the creator has designed through the transformation of the mind. How we stand in the evil day is very important for a successful outcome. For the outcome to be successful we must stand in righteousness.

In the past, we were caught up in lies; but now righteousness will have us rooted in truth. As our minds are fixed on truth we are covered by a reality that will develop through our feet being prepared with the gospel of peace. This good news builds hope and increases our faith. However, we must make sure that our mind is focused on our salvation during this process. The spirit will be our weapon to fight off the enemy to our future, because the word of God will give us directions on how to advance toward our dreams.

True happiness is bliss that can be enjoyed when we allow the dream to go to the extreme. We can experience ecstasy when we adhere to our spiritual needs and reject our physical needs. This is what the Bible describes as walking in the spirit. By delighting in the law of God we can experience euphoric living that is unknown to those that do not strive to reconnect with their purpose. Once our purpose become a desire to reconnect to the creator of the universe the creator helps erase the thought of past mistakes as we walk by faith and not act based on fear of the past or leaving our comfort zone. Jesus said all things are possible to them that believe. (Mark 9:23) He was speaking to the father of a boy possessed with a "dumb spirit". The amazing thing about this scripture is that in the next verse the father gave the same response many of us might have: "Lord I believe but help thou my unbelief." (Mark 9:24) This step requires being bold enough to say no to the past and this time the no must be for real. We want the all things are possible mentality to direct our faith walk.

Blessed is the man that walketh not in the counsel of the ungodly, nor standeth in the way of sinners, nor sitteth in the seat of the scournful. But his delight is in the law of the Lord; and in his law doth he mediatate day and night. And he shall be like a tree planted by the rivers of water, that bringeth forth his fruit in his season; his leaf also shall not wither; and whatsoever he shall prosper.

Psalm 1:1-3

LIVING THE DREAM

So God created man in his own image, in the image of God created he him; male and female created he them.

Genesis 1:27

In order to live the dream we must become intimate with the dream. This intimacy is acquired when we walk by faith and don't react with fear. The book of Genesis teaches man's original purpose was to take on the image of God, by being fruitful, multiplying and replenishing the Earth. Disobedience to the creative word of God has caused man to be dependent upon lies, and this refusal to obey the creative word has started a dysfunctional behavioral pattern. This pattern of behavior has continued to affect us now, and the only hope we have of not dying with this falsehood is by accepting the new life that comes by not being afraid to change. By living the dream, we are walking in faith and not reacting to circumstances by fear.

The book of Genesis is great for observing various patterns that have caused us so much discomfort in our lives. If our needs are continuously met by lies we will continue to be distracted from the image of God.

Genesis 1:31 relates that God saw everything that he had made, and behold it was good. The amazing thing about God is that he is the creator and if what he made was good then there is an experience that accompanies his words. This is the secret that the enemy to our dreams does not want us to know; this experience with God can be taken to the extreme. We aren't aware of this fact because many of us spend too much time emotionally attached to a lie. If we reversed the curse which came from this false belief, then we will get relief from this horrible grief. The reverse of this process is to start developing behaviors that will make us dependent upon the creator. We must have repeated interaction with our creator, not just a one-time experience. These interactions will develop emotional attachments and we will continue in our efforts to be like the creator. We will constantly create solutions to everyday problems. When depression and negative mental aggression tries to still our joy, because we walk in the spirit this can be replaced by the fulfillment of knowing that all things are working together for our good so we can't be defeated on reaching our goals.

I am the Lord, and there is none else, there is no God beside me: I girded thee, though thou hast not known me: Thou they may know from the rising of the sun, and from the west, that there is none beside me, I am the Lord, and there is none else. I formed the light, and create darkness: I make peace, and create evil: I the Lord do all these things.

Isaiah 45:5-7

Once we refocus on the image of the creator we will understand through experience that there is no other god like the true and living God. We will know him by the closeness that comes once we draw nigh to him he will draw nigh to us. Then we will develop an understanding of his ways and that he created the darkness so he could be our light. Once we understand him as our light we become familiar with the negative pattern that tries to distract us from the light. A relationship forms when we wrap our minds around his will for our lives which is the dream that directs us towards our destiny. This helps us become confident that our intimate relationship with the master will blossom into a pattern that replaces fear and activate faith in our destiny.

As we live our dream we must reflect on the God that has created us in his likeness and once we do this we will experience that which is good. The Bible mentions in Genesis 1:31 that "God saw everything that he made, and behold, it was very good." We have endured a lot of bad things in our lives and some blame a lot of these experiences on God.

First, we must continue to focus on the image of God. His reflection becomes clear when we start recognizing our goals as the will of God that can only be known through his word. Then we must act out his word because his word will direct us in the direction we need to travel to make our dreams a reality. Once we are walking in this direction we are living the dream. We are proof that God that has looked at his creation and declared it as good. Not only do we reflect this in our lives but we experience the goodness of God. The Bible invites us to taste and see that the Lord is good and that his mercies endure forever. (Psalm 34:8)

We must fall in love with the dream for us to take it to the extreme. This only happens when we fall in love with the one that has given us the ability to develop the ideas in our mind. Thoughts produce beliefs that result in actions, and again these actions are experiences that help us to know the Lord in an intimate way.

I am the Lord, and there is none else, there is no God beside me: I girded thee, though thou hast not known me: That they may know from the rising of the sun, and from the west, that there is none beside me. I am the Lord, and there is none else. I form the light, and create darkness: I make peace, and create evil: I the Lord do all these things.

Isaiah 45: 5-7

A way to replace the images of the past is to focus on a positive image. God has created us in his image. He wants us to be fruitful, multiply and replenish the earth based on this concept. We acknowledge some mistakes from the past but we must understand that evil was created by Lord. Yes, it's ironic but evil is designed for us to draw nigh to God so he can draw nigh to us.

> *I have sworn by myself, the word is gone out of my mouth in righteousness, and shall not return, That unto me every knee shall bow, every tongue shall swear.*

> Isaiah 45:23

> *Every valley shall be exalted, and every mountain and hill shall be made low: and the crooked shall be made straight, and the rough places plain; And the glory of the Lord shall be revealed, and all flesh shall see it together; for the mouth of the Lord hath spoken it.*

> Isaiah 40: 4-5

A new model of thinking must be developed in our minds to fight the fear. We should be intoxicated with the dream that comes from the heavens. Again, it replaces the negative thinking that leads to depression and an anxious state of mind. This replacement brings down the mountains that have confused us throughout life. It exalts us in our low points because now we have hope in the times that are evil, because we know this is the time to become intimate with the creator. Instead of being like Eve in the Garden of Eden and becoming inquisitive about the lie, we rely on our relationship with the master that can bring us out of any disaster. As we live like this our crooked paths become straight and our rough places become plain because we are walking in the glory of the Lord. Remember God said when he made his creation that it was good and now when we walk in his glory all flesh shall see it. Why shall all flesh be able to see the glory of the Lord? Again, His word has gone out, but before it went out God swore by himself that his word would not return without accomplishing its purpose. A perfect example of that is the life of Jesus Christ. Isaiah 40 explains how the word of God that was manifested in flesh, which allowed the glory of God to be manifested and was seen and recognized as the move of God. Now we must remember as we live the dream, we are actually living the lifestyle that the word of God portrayed as his word dwelt among men, and once this is done the dream goes to the extreme. Once God breathe into man and he became a living soul the dream was deposited into his system, now we must reconnect with the God that deposited his spirit in us. Once this reconnection takes place we walk in understanding that we are the creation that God looked at and said was good, but we must allow his image to subdue and have dominion over our negative thinking. We must not forget the fear that draws us away from God the creator and once we are drawn away it leads to depression and anxious states that cause many problems in life. Therefore, we cannot afford to forget that temptation comes from the thought of evil. This thought causes us to be drawn away from God if we are walking in the flesh. Once we are drawn away we delight in the negative sight, which weakens our will to say no to yielding to the fear that is produced by that which is spiritually not right. Once this act is committed we have just self- indulged in nothing which subtracts from us experiencing what God said about his creation being good.

> *Let no man say when he is tempted, I am tempted of God: for God cannot be tempted with evil neither tempteth he any man: But every man is tempted when he is drawn away of his own lust, and enticed. Then when lust hath conceived, it bringeth forth sin: and sin, when it is finished, bringeth forth death*

> James 1-13-15

God cannot tempt man with evil because evil was created by God for man to become intimate with him, because he wants us to turn to him in the time of tribulation so we can see the glory of the Lord. Also, he wants us to understand that he blew into us the breath of life and we became a living soul. This soul that longs for the creator discovers the creator when it is allowed to connect with the heavenly sent purpose. This is the dream which comes straight from the image in which we were formed. This image is God's likeness and once this is fruitful, multiplies and is replenished in our thinking daily we are living the dream.

Therefore, we cannot allow a response of fear to cause this dream to cease to exist, but we must walk by faith. This faith helps us experience the reality of God's promises that last forever. This extreme is what we should fight for, making God promises become realty in our life.

> *Yea, though I walk through the valley of the shadow of death, I will fear no evil: for thou art with me; thy rod and thy staff they comfort me.*

> Psalms 23:4

> *Therefore will not we fear, though the earth be removed, and though the mountains be carried into the midst of the sea;*

> Psalm 46:2

CONCLUSION

When God breathed into man and he became a living soul, and a dream was deposited with the soul to lead us to our destiny. Nothing can stop us from dreaming but fear from the negative past that can suspend our destiny. This negative past comes with experiences that haunt us. Jesus Christ birth, death, and resurrection, is the proof of why failure to reach our destiny is over. Acting and not wishful thinking relates to our destiny which is the mindset that we must develop in order to take our dreams to the extreme. The desire and opportunity lies within us but must be activated by faith and not the lust from within. This faith cannot be poisoned with self- indulgence into nothing because if we allow ourselves to chase nothing we experience the fact that nothing never adds up to something.

There is a dream killer that comes to steal our attention from the image in which we were created and if we allow this to happen we are responding in fear and not faith. By not walking by faith we surrender our ability to dominate and subdue negativity in our lives. We must not allow this dream killer to trick us with fear because his primary goal is to steal, kill and destroy our destiny. Therefore, we must constantly challenge ourselves to walk by faith and not act off of fear. Solomon mentions that the whole duty of man is to fear God and keep his commandments. (Ecclesiastes 12:13) As we reverence God this positive fear will not allow this dream killer to steal our spiritual identity because we have chosen to be precise with our vision that comes through trusting God's word to govern our life.

> *And the Lord answered me, and said, Write the vision, and make it*
> *plain upon tables, that he may run that readeth it.*

> Habakkuk 2:2

Once we identify through prayer the dream God will give us the steps to take it to the extreme, but we must remember to act based on faith. The acronym for faith is focusing always on inner spiritual thoughts that will make us happy forever. Many are searching following practices that guarantee death, but with God all his promises are forever.

We must accept that failure is not an option. We know that God's words will not return to him void. We can safely follow the words that proceed out of his mouth. This understanding should help us to find purpose in living for Christ so our existence will not end in death.

This renewed mind leads and guides us into all truth because we are walking in the spirit and not the flesh. Our God given purpose pursued through faith helps us to live the dream which comes from the image of God. We must remember that when God created everything he declared that it was good. We take the dream to the extreme by consulting God on his purpose for our life, and obeying his words so that we can enjoy the life that he has promised to give us more abundantly. Therefore, we must watch the experiences that define our reality because it transforms into being the good that God declared in the beginning of time. These experiences allow us to find purpose in drawing near to God.

> *Blessed are they that do his commandments, that they may have right to the tree of life,*

Revelation 22:14

Personal Refelction:

BASED ON YOUR PERSONAL GOALS THAT WAS LISTED FROM THE BEGINNING OF THE BOOK MAKE A LIST OF THINGS THAT YOU WANT TO CHANGE AND IDENTIFY A STRATEGY FROM THE BOOK TO CREATE AN ACTION PLAN TO HELP TAKE YOUR DREAMS TO THE EXTREME

PERSONAL GOALS (Dream)	ACTION PLAN (Taking it to the extreme)

ABOUT THE AUTHOR

D. Gatheright was born in Chicago, IL on November 10, 1972 to Jimmie and Torris Gatheright and is one of eighteen children. D. Gatheright has been married to the love of his life, Gabrielle Gatheright, for twenty-four years. They are parents to four wonderful children: Denisya, Dennis II, Gabriella and Gabriel. The family resides in Illinois.

D. Gatheright is the Junior Church Pastor and Associate Minister at Apostolic Assembly in Chicago IL where Bishop Jerry L. Jones Sr is the senior pastor. He has served faithfully in various capacities at his church for over twenty six years. In June of 2012 he received his Master's Degree in Psychology from The Chicago School of Professional Psychology. D. Gatheright is a High School English teacher and Case Manager at Crete-Monee Educational center in Monee IL. D. Gatheright has worked for the Chicago Public Schools for thirteen years. Along with teaching, he has worked with inner city programs and various social service agencies for over twenty years. He is a motivational speaker, gifted orator in addition to this book he has also published two other books, "Spiritual Sense" and "Replacing the Addiction." For more information on this "Motivational Author" please visit dgatheright.org.

REFERENCES

Unless otherwise stated all scripture references are taken from the King James Bible.
Sun Tzu, Samuel B. Griffith, The Illustrated Art Of War, Duncan Baird Publishers New York, New York, 2005